# A Beautiful Thing

## Uncontainable Worship

By Gillian Brebner

Cover Photo: Johanna Brebner

Edited & Co-Published by WordWyze Publishing
www.WordWyze.nz

A catalogue record for this book is available from the
National Library of New Zealand.



Printed Soft-cover Edition: ISBN-13: 978-0-473-53186-7
Epub Edition: ISBN-13: 978-0-473-53187-4

# Dedication

This book is dedicated to Jesus,
who alone is worthy.
And to those who are devoted to Him.

# Contents

Foreword

# Meeting the Presence

I love to worship. Probably because I first met the God of Christianity through worship.

I was in my mid-twenties, and for almost fourteen years had been searching for answers to some big questions about life. I wondered if God was real; I wondered what happens when we die; and I wondered what the purpose of life was. My quest had been launched by the pain of personal tragedy, and I explored diverse pathways hoping to find what my heart needed. But nothing satisfied my deep hunger.

A couple of times over those years, when I was alone in the beauty of creation, I became aware of a Presence much greater than myself. A Presence who gave me a supernatural peace which I knew was not my own, and which touched me so deeply that I knew it was the One I was looking for. But who was this One? How did I get closer and get to know him? Her? It? Was it Mother Nature? All I knew, was that this Presence changed the atmosphere, touched my heart, and was bigger than me.

Occasionally, I would go into an empty church and just sit. Alone in the silence. Aware of the gentle ebb and flow; echoes of weddings and funerals, worship and prayer, the human and the Divine in a creative dance. I could sense the faint peace of the Presence, but I never experienced it as strongly as I had outdoors in the beauty of creation.

I ventured into the occasional church service to see if I would find the Presence there. I heard a lot about God in those services, but I certainly never found Him to be real. If He was supernatural, then where was the evidence of His supernatural power when His people got together? All I experienced was people. Lovely people, yes, but I was seeking more than that. I was seeking to meet this Presence.

When I finally reached a place of complete desperation - when all the wheels seemed to be falling off in my world, I went one more time to a church. It was a little church down the road, in a little supper room, in a little hall, in a little town, in our little nation of New Zealand. And I walked to it, head down, in my raincoat and gumboots in the pouring rain. My inner world seemed as bleak as the muddy, wet, cold day around me.

The people were lovely. I was welcome. The guy who was leading the songs told us he was hugely nervous, as it was his first time doing this. I felt relieved. I felt nervous myself, so could relate to his pain.

There was a lady at the piano and only about fifteen people in the congregation. I felt very conspicuous as 'the visitor.' I was totally out of my comfort zone, but as we began singing it was a relief to find I knew two of the songs; The National Anthem and Amazing Grace. But what was not comforting, was that I began to feel odd things happening in my body. My flesh began to respond to something I could not see.

As thc singing continued, a Presence began to melt me. Firstly, my knees began to go weak. This had never happened to me before, and I had no idea what was going on. I was a fit, strong, healthy, very athletic young woman, yet I was having trouble standing. In fact, my legs got so weak that I had to sit down, much to my dismay. What would these people think about me sitting down in the middle of their singing?! Especially when my sitting down was very obvious as they were all still standing. But my legs would not co-operate. I was a sitting duck.

Then it got worse. Tears began to roll down my cheeks as my heart began to realise that this Power greater than I, this Presence who was exquisitely melting my physical strength, this Love that was overshadowing my soul, was the Christian God. *This was Him!* This was the One who had met me in creation, and I knew it. I recognised the atmosphere of His Presence, and it was all too much. I was completely undone physically, emotionally, and spiritually. I sat in a glorious, tearful, overwhelmed-by-His-Presence homecoming. This was the supernatural God whom I had heard of, and whom I had sought. And He met me in worship. This was my home. His Presence was where I belonged.

I never looked back. I absolutely knew from that one encounter that I had met the God of Christianity. Two weeks later, I publicly committed my life to Him, and my whole world changed. It went from blurry sepia tones to vibrant colour. It was the beginning of the wildest journey I have ever been on, yet even in the most difficult moments I have known His reality. I know what I have found, or perhaps I could more truly say, I know what found me. God. And the more I know Him, the more I love Him.

I guess because I came to know God through worship, I have always had a special place for worship in my heart. From experience, I know the kind of supernatural encounters that are possible when we worship our Christ. I am eternally grateful for the little group of people whose humble offering of worship opened the doors of heaven for me in that little church service that day.

This book comes from my own heart of devotion which has been captivated by Christ. I find no greater pleasure in this world than to encounter Him over and over again through worship, in whatever form that may take, whether that happens in a church, on the beach, while vacuuming the floor, or sitting in my garden. He is worthy.

This book is based on one little portion of Scripture which has come alive to me over time. It is not about the technicalities of corporate worship, or how to do this or that in a church service, it is simply about the heart of a devoted worshipper, whom Jesus singled out for our remembrance. Her name was Mary, and she lived at Bethany.

# Author's note

Matthew, Mark, and John write of a woman anointing Jesus at Bethany (Matt: 26:6-13; Mark 14:3-9; John 12:1-8). John alone identifies her as Mary of Bethany. There is some scholarly debate around the identity of this woman. Some believe the anointing in John is by a different woman to that in Matthew and Mark, but I believe that it is the same woman in all three accounts, and write this book from that perspective. My intention is not to get entangled in scholarly debate, but simply to capture the heart of this woman and her actions.

What stands out to me in the Matthew and Mark accounts, is that Jesus specifically stated that her story would be told and remembered.

This book is written in honour of His words.

# The Anointing at Bethany

*6 And when Jesus was in Bethany at the house of Simon*
*the leper, 7 a woman came to Him having an alabaster flask*
*of very costly fragrant oil, and she poured it on His head as*
*He sat at the table.*

*8 But when His disciples saw it, they were indignant,*
*saying, "Why this waste? 9 For this fragrant oil might have*
*been sold for much and given to the poor."*

*10 But when Jesus was aware of it, He said to them,*
*"Why do you trouble the woman? For she has done a good*
*work for Me. 11 For you have the poor with you always, but*
*Me you do not have always. 12 For in pouring this fragrant*
*oil on My body, she did it for My burial. 13 Assuredly, I say*
*to you, wherever this gospel is preached in the whole world,*
*what this woman has done will also be told as a memorial to*
*her."*

*Matt 26:6-13 (NKJV)*

Chapter 1

# Mary of Bethany

Mary of Bethany is a marvel. I am attracted to Mary and find my heart resonating with her. This woman always seems to come to the fore in the context of pure worship. She is either at Jesus' feet in devoted adoration, or lavishly anointing him.[1] She just cannot seem to help but be overtaken by the exquisite presence of her Lord, and to say 'yes' to the prophetic timing of the Kingdom at work in the moment. Mary is one who 'gets it.' This is no small thing when you consider that the twelve disciples often seemed to miss it.

This is the same Mary who was drawn to sit at the feet of Jesus, totally immersed in His presence, while her sister, Martha, industriously laboured in the kitchen with increasing frustration until she vented at Jesus.[2] When Mary is together with Jesus, it seems to irk people. In fact, more often than not, it irritates, offends, or even infuriates them.

This is the same Mary who lived at Bethany, and whose brother Lazarus was raised from the dead. She understood life and death, and knew Jesus better than most because she had experienced his intimate presence and power at work in her life as few do. We can learn a lot from Mary, and I am convinced that Jesus' strong intention was that we would, not only back then, but right now. In fact, I believe *especially now.* Mary's life reveals timeless keys to worship that matter right now in the western world.

Through Mary, God gives us an invitation to let go. Let go of our need to fit the agenda and timing of man and religion. Let go of the need to look good outwardly regardless of what's happening on the inside. Let go of offering worship in form and structure, but with truant hearts. Let go of our need to control. Let go of our man-made gospel.

But will we let go?

Mary brings us back to the heart of the gospel, which can so easily be smothered by the rampant vines of everything other than the simplicity of devotion to Jesus. She cared about Him, really cared about Him, over and above everything else. She demonstrated worship fuelled by relational set-apartness; her ear was His, her time, her possessions, her reputation and her future.

We need to learn from Mary. Mary matters.

## Chapter 2

# The Times

To grasp why Mary matters so much, we need to take another look at the crescendo of events surrounding Jesus' life just before this anointing took place.

The anointing chapter begins:

*Now it came to pass, when Jesus had finished all these sayings, that He said to His disciples, "You know that after two days is the Passover, and the Son of Man will be delivered up to be crucified."*
*Matt: 26:1, 2*

The anointing by Mary takes place on the eve of the crucifixion. The time has come. Jesus has set His face towards Jerusalem and knows that He will die there. In fact, He knows more than that, He knows He will be condemned to death, mocked, scourged, and crucified, but He also knows He will rise again.[3]

The devil, of course, has wanted Him dead from the beginning, and orchestrated many attempts at His life, ranging from Herod's demonically fuelled slaughter of all the boys under two years old in the Bethlehem area, through to Satan's face-to-face attempts at the Son of God in the wilderness temptations, through to the relentless blood-thirsty manhunt of Jesus by the religious leaders determined to obliterate Him.[4] At this point in the narrative, the wrath and envy of these leaders has increased to boiling point, in their poisoned pursuit of Jesus.

Jesus knows this, and far from being intimidated, He takes them on. Three chapters earlier, Jesus openly spoke to the multitudes and disciples with white-hot truth about the scribes and Pharisees.[5] Jesus never did march to the rhythm of man's agendas, least of all those wanting to kill Him. Their religious cover is well and truly shredded, as Jesus goes straight to the heart of their hypocrisy and exposes it with unrelenting light. Yet, He still loves them and yearns for them to turn their hearts toward

Him. As He finishes verbally laying them bare, He weeps over Jerusalem and her unbroken record of killing the prophets. Judgement is upon her, and He longs for it to be different. He longs for her to turn; for her religious leaders to turn. He always prefers mercy over judgement but allows them to choose.

The religious system chooses; it prefers to kill the prophets and reject Jesus.

After His blistering exposé of the religious leaders, Jesus then spends time with His disciples in private, discussing the events of the end of the age, and how to live well as the Kingdom advances.[6] The disciples seem to be listening attentively, and trying to grasp what He is saying. At the end of His conversation, Jesus reminds them again, almost matter-of-factly, that He will be crucified in two days.[7]

&

## Religious Wrath

During this intimate talk with His disciples, it has been almost easy to forget that in the previous chapter, Jesus had severely shaken the hornets' nest of the religious system. We are about to see the outcome. They are swarming, seething, and ready to kill. They've been exposed, and they want Him dead. It doesn't matter how it is done, as long as it is done.

~

## The Plot to Kill Jesus

*3 Then the chief priests, the scribes, and the elders of the people assembled at the palace of the high priest, who was called Caiaphas, 4 and plotted to take Jesus by trickery and kill Him. 5 But they said, "Not during the feast, lest there be an uproar among the people."*
*Matt 26:3-5*

The devil's handiwork through these religious leaders is chilling. Here is total confirmation of Jesus' scathing words about these same leaders' three chapters earlier. They are indeed like a "brood of vipers and whitewashed tombs". Murderers, masquerading as moral men, they have all the trinkets, baubles, bells and whistles of their religious system, but they are full of nasties.

And Jesus had just provoked them.

In typical Jesus-fashion, He confronted them face-to-face with His previous statements, "Woe to you, scribes and Pharisees, hypocrites!" "....blind guides!" "...fools and blind!" "...serpents, brood of vipers!"[8] He is no wimp. In fact, his courage astounds me. Who would do that? Who would openly pull back the corner of the rug of religion, in front of the multitudes, and one-by-one expose the evils which had been hidden in the darkness there? Expose the corruption, not just of the system, but of the hearts of the leaders? Who would do that?

Jesus would do that.

## Untameable

Jesus would do that because He hates anything that keeps people away from Him, and thereby limits their life. Jesus came to give us life in abundance. The thief comes to steal, kill and destroy. It is very easy to see which side the religious leaders of the day were on, and it wasn't on Jesus' side. Their religious system had the bulk of Israel by the throat, and Jesus had come to break that stranglehold. They might have been after Him, but He was in no way dancing to their tune. He was on a mission of liberation, throwing open prison doors with compassion, authority, and power wherever He went. Jesus cannot be tamed and never could be; not in the past, not in the present, nor in the future. Jesus remains perfectly free and offers that freedom to every follower. But it is contested. At times furiously and murderously contested.

Just before Mary's anointing, the religious leaders are found plotting deception and murder. So much for their righteousness. They were indeed children of their father, the devil, who was a murderer from the beginning and the father of lies.

Just as Jesus said.[9]

He certainly told it as it was. The verses are almost bizarre, as we find the leaders assembled at the high priest's palace, no doubt a place of opulence, and no doubt fitting to leaders used to upper-class life, being men of high standing in their society. Outwardly, they had it all; prestige, righteousness, holiness, reputation, power and intellectual elitism. Yet inwardly, and secretly, a foul brew of murder and deception bubbles up amidst them like sulphurous mud pools in a rotting swamp.

And it gets even more bizarre as they reveal their bondage to the fear of man – they want to avoid murdering Jesus during the feast, in case there is an uproar among the people. They don't want to attract the attention of Rome.

They are more scared of Rome than God, even though they are plotting to murder God's Son.

Absolute fear of man. Zero fear of God.
Bizarre.

## Mary

And into this brew steps Mary.

In contrast to this atmosphere of potent evil, the scene abruptly shifts to the home of Simon the leper, in Bethany. His home would be quite a transition, no doubt, from the finery of the high priest's palace. Indeed, switching to the home of a man identified by the word 'leper' could not be more of a contrast. Lepers were considered religiously unclean, banished from cities and sent to live in isolated communities. They were as low as it gets. Outsiders. Unwanted. Rejects. They would definitely never be found in the High Priest's palace, nor in the temple, not even in the outer courts. They were avoided and religiously excluded, as it was believed they polluted anything holy.[10] But it is at Simon's house that we next find Jesus, the Holy One.

Here, we find a bunch of them having supper; Jesus, the disciples, Lazarus, Martha and Mary. It seems like a homely and friendly everyday scene. Some are at the table with Jesus. Martha is serving. It is interesting to find this, as earlier, Jesus had specifically commended Mary for sitting at his feet, in contrast to Martha's industrious, and increasingly bothered, serving. [11] One would hope Martha had learned from that gentle rebuke of Jesus, in which Mary's act of quiet devotion had been chosen as 'better' by Jesus, yet here is Martha serving again. Then again, Martha was perfectly fulfilling a social norm.

Norms can be hard to break, and no doubt, this norm was firmly enmeshed within the wider cultural context. A woman's role in Israel at this time was typically domestic and subservient to men. A good woman would be expected to serve the men supper, just as Martha was busily doing. And norms have their place; supper was going smoothly.

But then, Mary does it again.

She breaks the norm.

And while individual norms of busyness are hard to break, cultural norms are *very*, *very*, hard to break.

Unless you're Mary.

Chapter 3

# The Anointing

*...a woman came to Him having an alabaster flask of very costly fragrant oil, and she poured it on His head as He sat at the table. Matt 26:7*

Mary just seems to have a knack for breaking norms. I don't think it's because she intends to break norms, I think it is simply because she is a Spirit-led lover of Jesus. She encounters Him, and it just happens.

She suddenly enters the supper scene armed with fragrant oil, then seemingly without even a moment's hesitation, she love-bombs on Jesus. This is totally unexpected behaviour, which at first appears wildly out of context. The nice supper becomes transformed by this collision of passionate worship against 'normal behaviour at suppertime.' And the whole atmosphere now changes.

The gospels of Matthew and Mark say Mary anoints Jesus' head, whereas John says it was His feet. Perhaps Mary was just so lavish with her anointing that it simply went everywhere.[12] Perhaps Jesus had it running off his hair, down his face, over his robe and onto his feet. Considering that she used a pound of the perfume (which is very close to our modern pound in quantity i.e. half a litre), she sure had plenty to splash around. And this was costly perfume. Top-of-the-line and heady.

*Then Mary took a pound of very costly oil of spikenard, anointed the feet of Jesus, and wiped His feet with her hair. And the house was filled with the fragrance of the oil.*
*John 12:3*

Sometimes, a woman wearing a dab of quality perfume can be smelled ahead of time, as she approaches down the street. Here in Simon's house, all the mouth-watering smells of supper would, most likely, now be completely engulfed by the overpowering scent of perfume. The whole house smelt like a perfumery, with no escaping the fragrance. Mary had not done a half-hearted job.

It would seem she had never intended to do a half-hearted job either. She had come in, armed with an enormous amount of top-of-the-line perfumed oil, which was a prized luxury cosmetic, and also sometimes used to anoint the dead. All three gospel writers make the point that it was 'very costly,' and Mark and John identify it as oil of spikenard or perfume of pure nard, worth approximately 300 denarii, which was the equivalent of one year's wages for a worker.

One year's wages! What was Mary thinking?! If we bring that into current New Zealand context, a year's average wage is somewhere around $50,000.[13] Mary, in one lavish outpouring, spends a year's wages on Jesus. Her heart is just astounding, and this whole scene is breath-taking. I don't think Mary was wealthy by the standards of her day; it was probably more likely that her income was well below average, and this makes her actions even more wondrous. She pours, literally pours, $50,000 of fragrance over Jesus.

On top of this, according to John, she ups the ante, and wipes Jesus' feet with her hair. This really is getting quite messy. Again, what was she thinking?! It was not a done thing, and still is not, for a woman to wipe a man's feet with her hair, especially in public at suppertime. *Especially* a rabbi's feet. It is quite scandalous. Definitely not normal. I guess it's a good thing that Mary wasn't concerned about being normal. In comparison to the Pharisees and their oversized fear of man, Mary seems completely free of it.

So now, Jesus is liberally anointed with perfume, Mary's hair and hands are covered with it, no doubt her clothes and the floor are splattered with it, and the whole house is filled with the fragrance.

Spectacular.

I don't believe Mary was trying to be spectacular though, or trying to draw attention to herself. It's simply that her extravagant love for Jesus upsets the apple cart each time. Whether it's here in the house with the disciples or in the earlier incident where Martha is caught up with distractions, Mary is simply being Mary. She 'gets it' about who Jesus is, and like a water-loving child, she just can't help but to jump right in the deep-end of His presence. And the waves and splashes of her demonstrative devotion soak the people on the banks and dangerously rock other people's nice safe boats.

And their norms and their nice safe boats don't like being rocked.

As Mary was about to find out.

Again.

## Chapter 4

# Waste

*'But when His disciples saw it, they were indignant, saying, "Why this waste?"*
*Matt 26:8*

Mary obviously hadn't thought too much about what people would think at the time. In fact, what do *we* think all these centuries later? What was our first thought when we read the value of the perfume? Did a stream of images parade through our imagination of how we could spend $50,000? An extravagant holiday, a new car, furniture, or luxury clothes? Or maybe how much of our mortgage we could pay off? Then again, maybe how much we could give away to the poor and needy?

$50,000 is quite a juicy sum to get one's hands on, and here is Mary opening her hands and so generously pouring it all out on Jesus. This extravagant act inevitably brings some hidden things to the surface in our lives. It reveals our hearts and exposes our idols. Like jack-in-the-boxes they spring into sight, and surprise us if they have been stuffed down deep in our hearts, where we have been unsuspecting of their existence. Our reactions can be remarkably out of proportion…

…just like the disciples.

The disciples, as one, are indignant. This has disturbed their dignity and provoked their anger. Their offence and derision are immediately evident in their scathing comment, "Why this waste?" They sound like belligerent bosses demanding answers. What the disciples don't realise, as many of us didn't if we had the same initial response as them, is that this question simply exposes how badly they missed it…

*"Why… this…* ***waste?****"*

These words are chilling. Close to icy cold.

They *missed it.* Completely.

What their words reveal is that they thought Jesus wasn't worth the devotion that Mary displayed.

Waste is defined by paying more than what we consider something is worth. If we know that a loaf of bread is worth $3 and yet we pay $5, it will be considered a waste, even more of a waste if we pay $10, a terrible waste if we pay $100, a tragic waste if we pay $1000 and an unthinkable waste if we pay more than that. We consider waste in proportion to the worth of the item.

Or in this case, the worth of a person.

That person being the Son of God.

Here, the disciples are basically saying that the Son of God is not worth $50,000. Mary's offering is too much to be wasted on Jesus. Oh, how badly they miss it. Big time. Here is Jesus, King of the Universe, Lord of Hosts, God in the flesh – Emmanuel; God with us, and the disciples decide the anointing is wasted on Him. He is not worth it.

The created judge the Creator as unworthy. Oh, dear.

## Worthy

What they have entirely failed to see is that Mary *got it.* She got a glimpse of who Jesus was. A glimpse is enough to cause you to do things like Mary did. It seems she was tuned into the realities of the Lord and His Kingdom because her worship was totally appropriate by the standards of that realm.

Worship around the heavenly throne can only be described as extravagant. Some of the prophets saw into, and experienced, these heavenly realms, seeing everything from the Lord himself to angels and celestial beings and the throne of God. Usually, they were unprepared for the extravagance and their bodies and minds short-circuited during their encounters. The results of these encounters included finding themselves face down on the ground, speechless, trembling, with no strength, undone, falling at His feet as though dead, totally messed up, and even physically blinded for three days.[14] It was all too much.

Inevitably, they struggled to find words to describe these experiences, and inevitably, these encounters marked them for life. The extravagance around the throne includes living creatures, elders and myriads of angels, and they're all lifting their voices in continual unity of worship proclaiming… "*WORTHY* is the Lamb!" Mary's actions indicate that she knew this in the Spirit; she knew who Jesus really was, that He was *worthy* of the worship around the throne of God, and absolutely *worthy* of a $50,000 anointing.

He was *WORTHY!*

## Backlash

Her worship session at Bethany, however, has come to a screeching halt in a spectacular collision. Unfortunately, the disciples are not finished with her yet. While she's there, they're going to let her feel the full weight of their misguided religious zeal.

*And they criticised her sharply. Mark 14:5.*

Or in other translations:

*And they rebuked her harshly. (NIV)*

*So they scolded her harshly. (NLT)*

Or as Eugene Peterson eloquently paraphrases it in The Message:

*Some of the guests became furious among themselves…They swelled up in anger, nearly bursting with indignation over her.*

As can be seen from these verses, Mary copped it for her act of devotion. She had ruined their nice little suppertime by being out of order according to their standards. Their reactions were instant and harsh. They were indignant and angry, and she was sharply rebuked, criticised and growled at. Mary was quite some woman to risk this type of verbal assault and do what she did. It just reveals even more, how much the disciples missed it. They considered the act a waste, and they considered her out of line.

She was personally attacked for her efforts. That's pretty intimidating stuff for a woman when she is in a decent-sized group of men. It's never pleasant being verbally assaulted, and even less so, when it is because of the ignorance and misunderstanding of those doing the assaulting. It is more bearable when we know we did something really out of line or wrong, but it hurts doubly when our heart has been totally misread. Somewhere along the way, it happens to us all, and it can be enough to shut us down.

It is perhaps one of the reasons that acts of devotion like Mary's are rare in the church these days. How many of us are prepared to make ourselves that vulnerable? Putting our devotion on display is an act of vulnerability. When we do it, we are basically saying, "Jesus, I love you so much that I'm going to demonstrate that love openly, regardless of the backlash." In our hearts, we know there will likely be a backlash because lavish demonstrations of devotion just seem to attract the ire of all camps. That's because the enemy can't stand anything that brings God glory.

*It takes a certain courage to be a Mary.*

The disciples obviously thought they were in the right about Mary because they came straight out with their verdicts. If they had harboured any inklings that she might have been doing something worthy, then they would have remained silent and allowed Jesus to speak first. Instead, they confidently voiced their unanimous censure of Mary. They were probably quite pleased with their discernment and protection of Jesus, fully believing they were doing the right thing. Many of us have probably walked in their shoes at some time.

These are the same disciples who had previously missed it badly themselves, having been caught up in misguided arguments about who was the greatest, and vying for the top leadership spot while walking with Jesus towards Calvary and His all-time act of humility and self-sacrifice[15]. A few days later, the three who were His closest friends still didn't grasp it, and fell asleep in the hour of his greatest agony at Gethsemane. In fact, Jesus seemed stunned by the degree to which they missed it; "What? Couldn't you watch with me one hour?"[16] The disciples didn't fare too well in those contested hours. They didn't have eyes to see. They all stumbled… "they all forsook Him and fled"[17] Despite adamant promises of allegiance, Peter explicitly denied Christ, and other wild reactions from the disciples ranged from severing a servant's ear by the sword, to fleeing naked.[18] So they had missed it before and were going to miss it again, but at this moment, they certainly thought they were right on the mark in berating Mary. Undoubtedly, to them, *she* had missed it.

And then there's the disciple, Judas, whose treacherous reaction is in a league of its own. For all time. Mary's act exposed Judas' idol of mammon and was the final straw for the man. He couldn't bear to see this level of extravagance poured out upon Jesus when it could have been pilfered into his own pocket. Of course, he didn't say that, he instead protested along with the others, that the perfume could have been sold and the money given to the poor. John's gospel, however, gives us the inside running of Judas' character; he didn't actually care about the poor, he was a thief, had the money box of Jesus and the disciples, and had been stealing from it all along.[19]

Judas was a lying traitor, and in his eyes, Mary's extravagant act of devotion was wasted on Jesus. Whatever other reasons he had for betraying Jesus, this was a tipping point for Judas. Both Matthew and Mark continue straight on from Mary's anointing, to tell us that Judas then went to the chief priests, and sided with them in their plot to murder Jesus. And he did it for the grand sum of thirty pieces of silver; approximately four months' wages, and the price of a slave.[20] This is what Judas considered Jesus was worth; the price of a slave. So, of course, Mary's act was a waste to him. He was determined to get his hands on money and feed his greed one way or the other. When our idols and false gods are confronted, we often have reactions far out of proportion, as Judas' ugly actions illustrate: he agreed to look for a convenient way to betray Jesus.

## Chapter 5

# Beautiful

We have heard the verdicts of the disciples and Judas. Their buckshot judgements have ricocheted around the room, but we have yet to hear from Jesus himself. Considering this act was done to Him and for Him alone, and He is the Son of God, it is His verdict which holds the weight of the universe. And what is His verdict?

> *"Leave her alone," said Jesus. "Why are you bothering her? She has done a beautiful thing to me."*
> *Mark 14:6a (NIV)*

"She has done a *beautiful* thing to me." What a captivating word - "beautiful." How much in the present context of Jesus' life was beautiful? Even focusing in on the anointing, how much was beautiful? The room was now full of harsh, critical, responses, and "beautiful" could not be a more direct contrast to the traitorous reaction of Judas, which was about to join ranks with the even uglier schemes conspiring among the religious leaders, outside the four walls of the supper room.

Even in our current context, how much is beautiful in the world today? Beauty can seem rare. Every day we are assaulted by local and international news which is dark. Often gruesome. Much of it absolutely evil; the fruit of ideologies which perfectly match the devil's agenda of cruelty, deception and murder.

Yet, here is Jesus commending this act as "beautiful." This makes my heart sing. Beautiful. Jesus, the Son of Man, covered in a mess of perfume, and He calls it a beautiful thing. I wonder how many other men would call such an act a beautiful thing. But this is His verdict. His masculinity was in no way threatened... He received it as *"a beautiful thing."*

Beauty seems to matter very much to God. If it didn't matter, then God could easily have cut corners and created an ugly world. It could have been an insult to the senses; glaring to the eye, painful to touch, bitter to taste, harsh on the ear, and a stench to the nostrils. Instead, He created it beautiful, and it invites us in. Despite the fall of mankind, and in areas we haven't yet ruined through war and exploitation, His fingerprints can still be clearly seen. And the original design is stunningly beautiful.

The exquisite beauty of creation is simply there because He made it to be. Natural, innate, radiating out from within. Like a child's innocent and captivating beauty. He loves beauty. We don't have to look far in New Zealand to see His creative eye for beauty. Our nation is stunning. Think of the scenery in Lord of the Rings; from crystal clear waters, to bush-clad wilderness, to towering, snowy Alps, to lush green pastures. Everything beckons us to dive in. The beauty is irresistible. It draws us closer.

Our Creator loves beauty. Even in the Garden of Eden, He was making things that were good to eat and pleasant to the eye. When it came to the tabernacle, He designed the garments of the priests for glory and beauty.[21] He didn't have to do that, but He obviously wanted to. Beauty means a lot to Him, and He calls Mary's act "beautiful." *"She has done a beautiful thing to me."*

## Good Work

The NKJV Bible translates these words slightly differently:

*"She has done a good work for Me." Mark 14:6a*

*"She has done a good work."* I find that interesting. I don't think I have ever heard it preached that we need to get on with good works like Mary's good work. When were you last encouraged to waste yourself in a splattered mess on Jesus?

The good works we tend to hear about are good works to people… feed the hungry, help the poor, clean the church, run a home-group, evangelise, visit the sick, and so on. We have so much work to do, it's not funny. Typically, there is more work to be done than volunteers to do it. In fact, church life can become a continual hamster-wheel going at ever-increasing speed with 'work that needs to be done.' And we never quite get there. We've hardly got over one project/course/whatever and another looms on the horizon. Many of us in the church are so busy working *for* Jesus, we have no time to spend time *with* Jesus. But here, Jesus redefines work.

Mary's act of devotion was "a good work." This might transform church life and discipleship a little. Jesus doesn't belittle feeding the poor, or any of the other works just mentioned, He simply elevates worship. We are not to put the poor above Jesus. Or any other thing above Jesus.

Worship is the ultimate act that He wants kept as the ultimate priority. And I'm not talking about worship teams doing their thing at church, but about intimate, personal acts of devotion and worship to Jesus himself, in private, or in public, individual or corporate. Not the perfectly clothed and choreographed performances we often witness in Western churches these days, which we call worship.

In fact, if we choose to learn from Mary, sit at the feet of Jesus, and to waste ourselves on Him in acts of devotion, we often no longer fit the wider church culture so well. The general focus on externals of 'nice Christian stuff' causes a restlessness that comes from hearts hungry for Him alone. We begin to see the busyness and the stuff as the blockages to true connection with God that they actually are. We begin to see the difference between church culture which centres on the church and Kingdom culture, which centres on the King.

By setting Mary and her act as a memorial, Jesus has sanctioned for all time, the type of worship He wants. It's innate. From the heart. Passionate. Free of the fear of men and full of the reverence and honour of God. It is centred on Him. Her act of devotion was free of the fakery of religious performance.

## True

Religious performance happens when our focus slips from God to ourselves. And it happens easily. It has probably happened to all of us at times, whereas Mary's focus is totally taken up by Christ. He has filled her sight and blown her fuses.

This type of worship is *true*. Her heart and her actions are in alignment, and she is the type of worshipper the Father is looking for.[22] He is actively on the lookout, seeking these types of worshippers with His eyes and ears tuned in. True worship is the opposite of fictitious or false worship. It is honest and *real.*

It is quite stunning to realise that scripture actually does speak of a type of worship that is indeed a waste of time. Considering that the disciples mistakenly disparaged Mary's worship as a waste, it is important to get an accurate understanding of what type of worship *God says* is a waste. In the words of Jesus:

> *'These people draw near to Me with their mouth,*
> *And honour Me with their lips,*
> *But their heart is far from Me.*
> ***And in vain they worship me…'***
>
> *Matt 15:8, 9a (highlights mine)*

*'In vain they worship me.'* To do something in vain means to waste one's time, energy, or effort for results that are empty and useless. The type of worship mentioned, in God's sight, was a complete waste of time because their hearts were not aligned with their lips. Honour and intimacy flowed from their mouths, but it was completely fake. Their

hearts weren't in it. And God knew it. They would have been better off to go and have a cup of tea.

I think we need to ask ourselves often, "Am I being real in worship?" We need to ask it individually, and to ask it as churches and ministries because I can think of nothing sadder than to continue merrily, but blindly, on in hypocritical worship, which is a total waste of time in God's sight.

This type of hypocritical worship is a little like the White Witch of Narnia. It has a chilling beauty. Carefully presented perfection on the outside, but cold on the inside. And harbouring deceptive motives. Just like the Pharisees who "appear beautiful outwardly, but inside are full of dead men's bones and everything unclean."[23] Also, a little like what the Western world commonly calls beauty – a forced external 'beauty' from ceaseless cosmetic surgery and slavery to fashion trends. These counterfeits of the word 'beautiful' are jaded comparisons to God's original design because over and above externals, true beauty originates from the heart.

## Hearts

Mary's actions overflowed from her heart. The word 'beautiful' as used by Jesus in this context of Mary's act, contained both an aesthetic meaning and an ethical meaning. In other words, what Mary did was beautiful both inside and out. Her action was beautiful, and her heart was beautiful.

Mary's worship was real because it was a response to revelation, and this is where all true worship originates. True worship cannot be manufactured, it is simply a response to revelation. We cannot actually figure God out with our intellects. We might use our intellects to help string things together, but it is only by revelation that we are given access into the spiritual realities of God and His Kingdom.

He reveals, and we respond.

The Creator reveals Himself to the created. This is illustrated elsewhere when Peter hits the nail on the head and professes Jesus as "the Christ, the Son of the living God." Jesus fills us in that Peter's recognition came purely through revelation.

"Blessed are you, Simon Bar-Jonah, for flesh and blood has not revealed this to you, but My Father who is in heaven."[24] Mary's extravagant act was in response to revelation. This type of worship comes spontaneously and is true.

True worship can be loud and demonstrative, such as King David dancing, leaping, twirling, and shouting before the ark after receiving the revelation that God was way holier than he realised. Or it can be completely still and silent, lost in adoration and immersed in communion with God. It is not the outward that defines true worship. Rather, it is that the outward and the inward are in alignment and true to one another. Clapping and shouting in an outward performance to God, but with a heart focused on self, is untrue, no matter how good the outward performance looks. And it can look pretty spectacular at times.

Equally, a stance of pious and silent reverence, if accompanied by a heart focused on self, is untrue. And often the only one who knows is God. "The Lord sees not as man sees; man looks on the outward appearance, but the Lord looks on the heart."[25] And what He sees is the most important.

In the case of Mary's act of devotion, He holds it up forever as "a beautiful thing." It was obviously an act of worship in spirit and truth that we can allow to inspire us into a deeper expression of worship ourselves.

In reality, though, what would we think if Mary did such a 'beautiful thing' in our church today? If it cut across the agenda, made a mess on our expensive carpet, interrupted the important people, splattered our Sunday-best clothes, and caused contention and complaints? We'd perhaps think "surely, that's not God."

God-honouring outpourings often appear inappropriate if we don't look with Spiritual eyes, listen with spiritual ears and keep our hearts soft and open, remembering that worship is not about us; it is about Him. Jesus' own words ought to be the greatest authority on the type of worship He is looking for, and we would be wise to heed his words to His disciples here.

Jesus received her anointing. He allowed himself to be love-bombed. He didn't tell her to get herself in order. He didn't turn her away or shut her down. He wasn't embarrassed at being covered in perfume in a demonstrative outpouring in front of the other blokes. He wasn't frustrated by this interruption right when He knew His time was short and He probably had much yet to teach and impart to the disciples.

The disciples tried to smother and bury the act, but Jesus received it. In fact, He enjoyed it.

And far more than that…
far, *far*, more than that…

*Jesus honoured it.*

## Chapter 6

# Memorial

Jesus honoured Mary's anointing. With a memorial.

> *"Assuredly, I say to you, wherever this gospel is preached in the whole world, what this woman has done will also be told as a memorial to her." Matt 26:13 (Words of Jesus).*

Memorials are intriguing things. In my own life, there are times I'm drawn to visit our local cemetery, and sit by the memorials of my cherished family members who have passed away. There, I contemplate life and death, and eternity. The fresh perspectives I gain never fail to enrich me.

Recently, as I sat there quietly pondering, my eyes began to wander slowly across the park-like surroundings. I was drawn to the variety of headstones and began to stroll quietly among them. There were the faded, barely readable, sad-looking memorials; just a name. No details. No messages of love or connection. The person's life apparently like a breeze that had wafted through existence and barely been noticed. Then there were the huge elaborate headstones that vied for prominence. Almost as if to demonstrate who had been the most important in life.

The headstones reminded me of a time when I was asked what I would like written on *my own* headstone. The exercise was designed to connect people to their deeper values in life and help them evaluate how they were doing in living out these values. It was a good exercise to give perspective this side of the grave and for sharpening focus. Yet over time, I felt it was only one side of the equation and missed the deeper realities of the Kingdom of God.

I felt it missed a deeper truth; it is not the human words said about us on our headstone that matter most, but rather the words of God spoken about us on the other side of the grave. It is not our send-off here that is the plumb line of our worth, but rather it is our welcome into eternal realms. It wouldn't surprise me if some of the greatest welcomes in heaven have gone to believers who were buried in unmarked graves on earth. People who were viewed by their fellow humans as 'the least,' and whose graves reflected that human judgement.

As my gaze ranged across the memorials and I pondered these thoughts, I sensed the Lord say,

"I know how to honour those who are mine."

He does indeed.

He knows how to create memorials of the highest honour. And that is exactly what He did for Mary. And He did it this side of the grave.

## Chosen

The reason Mary matters is that Jesus said so. He could have chosen the huge and elaborate temple for our remembrance, complete with its impressive religious leaders full of zeal for the Scriptures.

But He didn't.

He could have singled out any of His disciples to be remembered. In fact, it would have seemed more logical if He had chosen one of the three,

Peter, James or John, who seemed to be closest to Him and whom He chose to be with Him during His transfiguration, the raising of Jairus' daughter from the dead, and other such intimate and hidden moments.[26] He could have chosen any of the disciples' demonstrations of power such as when the seventy returned with joy, saying, "Lord, even the demons are subject to us in your name." [27]

But He didn't.

He chose Mary and her act of worship. In no way does this diminish the other disciples nor their deeds, but it certainly elevates Mary and what she did. There is *no-one else* in the Gospels for whom Jesus does this.

*No-one.*

He singles out Mary. Surely this should get our attention. If Jesus elevates this event so highly, He not only wants us to remember it, He wants us to learn from it.

## Remember

Memorials hold powerful lessons. They commemorate. When we get to them, we often find ourselves invited into other dimensions of time and place as they bring us face-to-face with mortality and eternity. They have the capacity to draw up emotions from the depths of our souls that catch us unaware. Often, in these places, God speaks and often also, we sense the voices of those who have faithfully run the race before us, voices from beyond the veil. It pays to have soft and receptive hearts when we ponder memorials so that we don't miss the messages they carry.

God's people of the Bible were familiar with memorials. Memorials were woven into their feasts and even their priestly garments.[28] The landscape of their nation was dotted with memorials in the form of stones which commemorated encounters with God, such as Jacob's heavenly encounter at Bethel and the Israelite's miraculous crossing of the Jordan River.[29] These memorial stones helped keep their stories of faith alive through the generations. The memorial stones sparked memories, invited questions, and prompted conversation. They learned from them.

We don't make memorials to things we don't need to remember. Memorials are about remembering. They are made in honour of what we consider worthy of remembrance; war memorials for our fallen soldiers; parks named after those honoured in the community; gravestones for those we have loved and cherished. Then there are memorials such as Israel's Holocaust Museum or Cambodia's Killing Fields Museum. Grim reminders of the darkest tendencies of humanity. Often, we would prefer not to remember. But if we turn away, we forget at our peril. These memorials beg us to learn from past mistakes. They beg us to *remember*.

The problem is, we can easily go rushing past memorials, caught up in the busyness of life and intent on building our empires, churches, and retirement funds. We can be so enamoured by the future, that the past can seem irrelevant, stale, and out-of-fashion. Indeed, to those who don't understand, memorials are just relics of bygone times to be left in the dust of our progress. They are silent witnesses that are often easily overlooked.

To those who do understand, however, they are timeless, and contain precious perspectives of wisdom for *now*. Memorials remind us of what matters. They are places to ponder messages from the past. They help us turn aside from the surface froth and bubble of life and look down into the still depths where we find keys and principles that are significant, often eternal. These speak through the generations, beckoning us to choose the path of Life, and bringing us back to what's important. Often, they bring us back to love.

## Red Letter

The astonishing thing about this particular memorial to Mary is that it was specifically chosen by Jesus himself, not society in general. This should be enough to abruptly turn us aside from lesser pursuits, in order to take a second look. What is it about this memorial? This memorial that Jesus wanted *permanently* joined to the gospel *wherever* it was shared.

*"...wherever the gospel is preached in the whole world...." v.13.*

Wherever and worldwide.

*"...what this woman has done will also be told as a memorial...." v.13.*

Permanently told along with the gospel.

For all time.

These instructions are the words of *Jesus Himself.* This is impressive. Christians so value the words of Jesus that some Bibles print His words in red to make them stand out. His words then draw the eye and become easier to find. This is done because we recognise that Jesus' words are life. It reflects our belief that the life, death, and resurrection of Jesus, the Son of God, is central to the Christian faith. So, Jesus' words, spoken as He lived amongst us for over three decades in human form on planet earth, have tremendous weight for those of us who follow Him. Even these millennia later, we drink of them as living water. They carry the voice of the One we love and to Whom we have dedicated our lives. To us, what Jesus says matters. It *really* matters.

We hang onto what He says, knowing that everything included in the Bible about Jesus' life, is God-breathed.[30] John tells us that if all the stories about Jesus were to be written individually, even the whole world probably couldn't contain them.[31] So we can know that the stories included in the Bible are of great importance. Nothing irrelevant is in the book.

Yet, even amongst all this God-breathed material, even amongst all the words of Jesus, so carefully highlighted in red and brought to our attention, is a particular event and a particular person He tells us to *remember.*

Mary.

In red-letter words.

## Sacred Cows

So, why is it that we seem to have let these words of Jesus, the Son of God, slip? I have rarely heard the memorial to Mary spoken of, not just with the Gospel, but anytime at all. And I don't think I am an isolated case. It seems to me that in the Western church, we have predominantly missed the memorial. How tragic! Perhaps it has been neglected, overlooked, or forgotten. Perhaps even avoided. Maybe it is because this story of Mary challenges so many sacred cows of church life, past and present.

Mary's anointing is not comfortable. It challenges stale tradition which needs no living movement of the Spirit, least of all, a Holy Spirit break-in as in this anointing. It challenges patriarchal ways which don't seem to think women particularly worthy of anything, least of all little-known Mary of Bethany. It challenges controlling ways which are offended by Mary's seemingly out-of-control display, so full of mess and spontaneity. It challenges lukewarm faith which finds anything spiritually on-fire too over-the-top, and it challenges the safe waters of reason and logic preferred by intellectual religion, which finds radical faith too 'out-there.' Mary's anointing just doesn't fit the mould of much Western Christianity and would likely be seen by many as an embarrassment to be moved-quickly-along-from-now.

Our desire in most streams and denominations of Christianity, through every era, to preach the full gospel seems to have missed something. Mary's story. It is not complete without this story. They are running mates. Yet, almost as one, we seem to have had our reasons why we'd rather not elevate Mary and her act. Jesus said this story was to be told wherever the gospel went, and He didn't just mean told once to get it over and done with.[32]

*I tell you the truth, wherever the Good News is preached throughout the world, this woman's deed will be remembered and discussed."*
*Matthew 26:13 (NLT)*

*Remembered and discussed.* He wanted this story told and re-told, talked about, and passed on. He wanted us to speak about it and for it to go viral with the gospel. It wasn't just to be recorded in Scripture and left at that. In the same way, the message of the gospel is not just left in the pages of Scripture for people to find, (though some do find the gospel that way), but is lovingly picked up from the written Word, and verbalised, shared, preached, and taught. In this way, it is carried to human ears by Spirit-filled human breath in the form of speech, and Jesus wanted this story carried in the same way.

## Timeless

Shortly before Mary's anointing, Jesus told the disciples that the Gospel would be preached to all men before the end would come.[33] And for better or worse it has been preached since then. Today, almost 2000 years have passed, but we still have people-groups that have not heard the gospel, so we know we are to continue. Jesus likewise intended for the telling of this story to continue until He returned because it was to accompany the gospel.

What this tells us is that this story carries timeless truths, just as the gospel does. This was not about Mary and the anointing being in vogue for a season. The gospel is always in season, and therefore this type of devotion is always in season.

At a certain level, we do see seasons in the Kingdom. For example, a particular worship song, ministry, gifting, or teaching may rise for a time. It will usher in new advances in specific areas of the Kingdom, and lift us to what the Spirit is currently highlighting and breathing into. These advances are marks of the times, but what we are talking about here regarding Mary is over and above all of that.

This is not about a season of something. Rather, Jesus wanted Mary and her act memorialised throughout time to show that this type of devotion is always 'in.' Mary's anointing is a practical example of true devotion. It is what we are to be saved into. It is at the heart of the gospel because the heart of the gospel is relational.

That Jesus wanted it told throughout "the whole world," also means it has timeless principles that supersede Jewish culture. These principles are relevant in the whole world, to all cultures because they supersede man-made culture, and communicate the culture of the Kingdom.

Jesus is also particular regarding what He wants talked about in this memorial.

*"Assuredly, I say to you, wherever this gospel is preached in the whole world, what this woman has done will also be told as a memorial to her."*
*Matt 26:13*

*"What this woman has done"* as *"a memorial to her."* It is not just about what she has done; it is also about who she was. He could have just said to remember what she had done, meaning her physical actions and behaviours, and left it at that. Instead, He also specified it was a memorial *to her,* meaning her person, her heart, the essence of this woman.

This is quite astounding. The only other person in the gospels that He told us to remember was *Himself,* "...do this in remembrance of me" which He did at the Last Supper when He inaugurated the New Covenant and instructed His disciples to *remember Him* through the bread and the cup.[34] Incredibly, He also wants us to remember Mary.

Jesus uniquely honours Mary, and this indicates that there is something special about her which He wants us to 'get.' Something that demonstrates the heart of the Kingdom of Heaven in a way Jesus wants immortalised and put into practice throughout the generations.

Chapter 7

# Prophetic

There is still the feeling that there is more to this memorial than meets the eye. A sense of mystery as to why this meant so very much to Jesus. Fortunately, Jesus provides insight to those who seek it.

*"For in pouring this fragrant oil on My body, she did it for My burial."*
*Matt 26:12*

He provides the clues to interpreting Mary's act for us. He is the one who knows our hearts, and we can trust that He knew Mary's heart and brought it into the open so that we would not be left second-guessing her actions.

ক

## Burial

He wants us to know that she did it for His burial.

She poured fragrant oil on His body in preparation for His burial. She 'gets it' that He is going to die, and He is going to be buried. Jesus has been telling the disciples this for a long time. Back in Matthew 16:21-23, when Jesus first began to show the disciples that He was going to suffer, die, and rise again, it was anathema to them. Thus, Peter rebuked Jesus and boldly cut across everything with his "no way!" to Jesus' plans. Followed by Jesus' abrupt silencing of Peter's well-meaning protest with those shocking words, "get behind me, Satan!"[35] It seems a harsh rebuke. Why was Jesus so severe with Peter? Perhaps, because Peter had unwittingly aligned himself with the things of men in opposition to the things of God. He had set himself against Jesus by wanting Him to avoid this path of suffering, death, and resurrection.

In the Kingdom of God, it is a grievous mistake to be, in the words of Jesus, "not mindful of the things of God, but the things of men."[36] Jesus calls Peter's act an "offence" or "stumbling block" to Him. In other words, Peter had got it so wrong that he was hindering Jesus. His error hindered the King. It is a sobering thing to realise that when we are mindful of the things of men rather than the things of God, we become an offence, a stumbling block, to God's plans.

In contrast to this, Mary 'got it' regarding God's plan. She was mindful of the things of God and aligned with His plan.[37] She was unafraid of death's intimidation. She anointed Him for burial and in so doing, proclaimed a resounding "yes!" to the Lord's plan. "Yes, and amen!" "So be it!" Not in a defeatist attitude, but in faith at certain victory over death. This was only hours or days before the crucifixion when the pressures of his impending torture and death were upon Him. At that crucial time, Mary came alongside Jesus with this incredibly powerful, prophetic act, and decreed by her actions in agreement with God's plans, "you will die, but you will rise in victory." She got it about resurrection, whereas Peter and the others still resisted it.

It is no surprise that Mary understood, as Resurrection was sitting at the table in the very same room with them, in the form of Lazarus, her brother. Jesus had ripped him out of the clutches of death and decay, not long before, with His realm-shaking command, "Lazarus, come forth!" To which Lazarus' rotting corpse arose and departed the tomb.[38] Mary understood death. She had had her heart ripped apart by the loss of her brother. She knew its cruel agony. But Mary had experienced more than this; she had experienced her beloved brother returned from death through the power of Jesus. She *knew* resurrection. Personally.

The disciples may have been slow to understand it all, but she had experienced it, and she knew it deep within. She knew that Jesus had power over death. This burial anointing was an act of victory.

An absolute bullseye of a prophetic act.

No wonder it meant so much to Jesus. Here was someone who got it, and who was with Him and for Him in faith, as He faced the hardest trial of all.

To top it off, in the upside-down way typical of God's Kingdom, He would go into this final apocalyptic battle - *the battle* of all eternity - covered in perfume and smelling either like a dead body or a woman. God has a sense of humour.

## Bethany

God also has a sense of warfare. He is *Yahweh Sabaoth*, the commander of the armies of God, Lord of the Angelic Host.[39] That this anointing occurred at Bethany was no accident. It was a prophetic act of warfare.

Bethany was a town two miles east of Jerusalem and the hometown of the siblings Lazarus, Martha, and Mary. In the final week before His crucifixion, Jesus spent a lot of time there with these special friends. Bethany was the very town in which Lazarus had previously been raised from the dead. Death had been publicly defeated here once already, and it was about to happen again at a whole new level.

In addition, it was the very town from which Jesus would ascend in the near future. In this very place, after His death and resurrection – in front of His disciples, while blessing them, He would be carried up to heaven before their very eyes. [40]

At Bethany.

Bethany seems to have quite a reputation. A place where death gets trumped. A place of resurrection power. A place of open heavens. Interestingly, John describes Bethany as the "town of Mary…"[41] Perhaps the extravagant worship and devotion of this woman contributed to the open heaven of this town? I wouldn't be surprised, considering that worship can be more powerful than a war party going out.[42]

## Humanity

Mary's act was also an act of cherishing the humanity of Jesus. Matthew and Mark say it was His head that was anointed, John says His feet, but Jesus doesn't seem too pedantic about details, He says she anointed His body. How beautiful a touch of mercy, compassion, love and honour. How much it must have meant to Him to have someone who actually honoured His physical body. He was, after all, a person like us, made of flesh and blood. While walking this planet, one of His favourite self-designations was the *Son of Man*.

Again, Mary's act is brought sharply into focus when we ponder what happened to His body shortly after this anointing. After being unjustly condemned, His body was scourged;[43] a barbaric practice which violently and mercilessly pulverised and ripped a person's flesh with whips which many never survived. He had a crown of thorns impaled and beaten onto His head, and His beard torn out.[44] He was mocked, slapped, had His face spat upon, was stripped naked, and crucified.[45] Crucifixion was and still is, one of the most heinously sadistic methods of torture and death invented. Sometimes victims remain alive and hanging in agony for days.[46]

Isaiah 52:14 says Jesus was marred beyond recognition.

How our Saviour suffered in His body. The torture He endured is sickening. Mind-numbing. Heart-wrenching.

Mary's stunningly beautiful anointing catches and radiates the light as an act of pure love against this looming backdrop of darkness and depravity.

Did the fragrance of the perfume stay with Jesus through His trial, torture, and death? Did it keep Him company in the garden of Gethsemane when all others failed Him? Did it remind Him at crucial moments when life and will waned, that victory was waiting on the other side of this last torturous mountain climb? Did "a beautiful thing" help carry Him through?

If not the fragrance, then at least the memory would be fresh to Jesus. We can only surmise, but one thing we do know, this act was incredibly precious to Jesus. "She did it for my burial." She honoured Him beforehand. He knew He was going to a death of dishonour reserved for slaves and criminals, but through it, He would carry this honouring touch of heaven and earth to Him as a person. The body of the Son of Man was valued.

And it doesn't stop there.

## *New Covenant*

Mary's anointing of Jesus' body is prophetic in an even deeper way. Matthew and Mark continue the story almost without break, into Jesus' introduction of the New Covenant during the Passover meal. And what does Jesus tell us to remember?

*His body.*

Mary had just focused all attention on His person, His body, in her anointing, and now Jesus Himself brings all attention again to His body. "Take, eat; this is My *body*" "… this is my *blood.*" Mary's act had been prophetic, and now Jesus shows us why her act was so totally on the mark - in timing and content. This was all about His body being given for us. The fulfilment of His earlier words "the bread I shall give is My flesh, which I shall give for the life of the world."[47] At the time of the anointing, He had told the disciples that Mary and her deed were to be remembered and now, shortly after, He tells the disciples to take the bread and cup to remember Him.[48] His body, His blood.

Mary had prophetically honoured this institution before Jesus set it in place.

Astonishing.

This is no doubt part of the reason Mary and her deed are to be remembered and told hand-in-hand with the gospel.

## Priest and King

And then there's the stunning reality that her act prophecies Jesus as both Priest and King.

Once again, Mary's anointing causes the windows of heaven to be flung open, and revelation poured out to us about who Jesus really is.

In the Old Testament, priests and kings were anointed to signify God's divine call and favour upon them.[49] In the New Testament, Jesus was the ultimate, divine fulfilment of these roles.

As the High Priest of the New Covenant, He replaced the old priestly order and sacrificial system. He was both the once-for-all perfect sacrifice for sin, and the new mediator between God and man. The book of Hebrews unpacks layers of revelation around Christ's priesthood surpassing that of Aaron's, in the Old Testament.[50] But here is Mary, years before the book of Hebrews was even written, anointing Jesus in an uncanny duplicate of the anointing of Aaron, in which the anointing oil was poured over his head, ran down his beard, and over the edge of his robes.[51]

Added to this, Jesus is King and all the kings of Judah were anointed before their coronation by prophets. While Mary is never alluded to as a prophet, her anointing carries the sharpness of a prophetic act… because Jesus is a king and He is about to be crowned. And here is Mary anointing him beforehand, as the prophets of old did to the Kings of Judah.

Jesus had been sought out as the King of the Jews by the magi at the beginning of His life on planet earth. Through the supernatural guidance of the Spirit in creation, they travelled from distant lands and were brought to the place He dwelled. These gentile magi recognised and worshipped Him as King of the Jews while He was just an infant.[52]

Nathanael, a Jew, was another who had 'eyes to see' and his inspired statement, "You are the King of Israel!" at his first meeting of Jesus, is astounding. Words of pure revelation from a man in whom there was no deceit.[53]

Now, at the end of Jesus' physical life on this planet and on the eve of his death, Mary's anointing undoubtedly confirms the worship of the magi and the words of Nathanael. It also foretells his coronation as the King of a Kingdom far more expansive than the physical borders of Israel. The Old Testament prophets spoke of this coming King. The King of Glory.[54] The everlasting King.[55]

In the New Testament, Jesus Himself announced at the beginning of His ministry, that the kingdom of God was at hand.[56] And a kingdom is ruled by a king. Jesus is the King of the Kingdom, and this Kingdom was made manifest as it began to overthrow the plans of darkness in a Divine revolution. Throughout His ministry, corrupt human kingdoms and unjust systems began to crumble; the broken and marginalised were raised up, demons were spectacularly evicted, and the banner of His love was unfurled with glorious grace.

Mary's anointing once again opens a portal between the realms. The Old Testament prophecies of the King of Glory, of the everlasting King, of the Son whose government would increase and have no end, are brought into the moment by her anointing, bursting to life in that very room through her prophetic outpouring. And as she lavishes her devotion upon the King, we can tilt our head and turn our ear towards the future, and hear this revelation picked up by Paul in his triumphant declaration a few decades later…

*Now to the King eternal, immortal, invisible, to God who alone is wise, be honour and glory forever and ever. Amen.*
*1 Tim 1:17*

For on the other side of Jesus' death came His resurrection, and in due time, came Paul's direct encounters with the risen Christ. From these encounters came Paul's ongoing revelation of Christ, which gains momentum even in this letter to Timothy. By the end of the letter, the King becomes more expansively described as

*…the King of kings and Lord of lords…*
*1 Timothy 6:15*

Jesus, the King of kings. He is not just any old king. He is *the* King of all kings. Not only a king of Israel or nations. No. He is the King of kings who holds all authority in heaven and on earth and under the earth. Totally, unreservedly, in a league of royalty unrivalled by any other being in the universe.

This supernatural and sovereign Kingship is brought graphically to life a decade or more later in the Apostle John's encounter with the King of kings. While in the Spirit John is taken into a vision where he sees Jesus as

*KING OF KINGS AND LORD OF LORDS*
*Revelation 19:16*

This King is definitely not one to be mucked around with. Faithful and True. The Word of God. The King of kings and Lord of Lords. He is no fluffy marshmallow. He leads the armies of Heaven. He is the King of Glory. He is the Lord of Hosts.

Mary's anointing prophesies this beforehand.

In one harbinger of an outpouring, she prophesies Jesus as the victor over death, His body as given for us, and as High Priest and King of

Kings. All of this suggests Him as the long-awaited Messiah, the *anointed one.*[57]

Astounding.

## Spirit

So why was there such opposition from the disciples towards Mary and her act of devotion? We have seen that the disciples regularly struggled, as we all do, in figuring out who Jesus really was.[58] As most of us have found, Jesus is more than a lifetime worth of figuring out. Just when we think we are getting a handle on who He is, we receive new revelation and realise we knew Him even less than we realised. He is so much more.

Even after living, travelling, and ministering together for three years, Philip, on the very eve of the crucifixion, revealed he still didn't really know who Jesus was, and Jesus seemed almost cut when He answered, "Have I been with you so long, and yet you have not known Me, Philip?"[59] This 'missing it,' however, does not fully account for the harsh anger of the disciples towards Mary.

What their opposition does expose, is another facet of the Kingdom of God which we tend to forget. Perhaps we forget because we do not tell and re-tell this story of Mary and hold it up as an example of Godly devotion.

What we forget, is that extravagant acts of Spirit-led Godly devotion will inevitably ignite opposition from the flesh. The natural man does not understand the things of the Spirit; in fact, those born of the flesh persecute those born of the Spirit. We only have to read Paul's book of Galatians to see that this battle is age-long.

The flesh majors on externals, whereas the Spirit majors on the heart. The flesh sticks to the law, likes comfortable boxes, is staunchly independent, and wants to look good. It very much likes to keep up appearances. What it does not realise, is "that those who are in the flesh cannot please God."[60] There is no simpler summary: walking in the flesh cannot please God.

We only have to look at the life of Christ to see this battle. To the flesh, the actions of the Spirit can appear out of rhythm, out of the norm, out of order, illogical and uncomfortable. We can see it in the life of Jesus. He would vanish from a town just as they wanted Him to stay; refused to be crowned king when the crowds were pushing for His coronation; remained silent when given an opportunity to speak before Herod; sometimes avoided the crowds for solitude; at other times waded into ministering to them; and at other times, veered off to an individual's home instead.[61]

The wind blows where it wishes, so is everyone who is born of the Spirit.[62] Jesus modelled this for us, and the collisions of flesh and Spirit that surrounded His life were obvious. The movements of Jesus were not choreographed by men's ideas, or human need, but by the Spirit of His Father.

It is not always easy to stay in step with the Spirit because it is a freedom that is opposed. While it is a freedom purposed by Christ for His followers, it is no cakewalk. It is the battle of promise, Spirit, and liberty, versus law, flesh, and bondage. We have to stand fast in it.

Staying in freedom takes deliberate decisions to always say 'yes' to the Spirit of God, regardless of the manifestations of flesh which might be provoked. Will we walk in the Spirit dependent on God's grace or in the flesh dependent on our own efforts? Will our priority be to please God? Or to please man?

The reactions of the disciples correspond to the way of the flesh. These followers may have walked with Jesus a few years, but their flesh is often still dictating, and they have yet to be filled with the Spirit. The Holy Spirit had not yet been given, as Jesus had not yet been glorified.[63] The Spirit is like the wind, and those who are led by Him are equally spontaneous, they carry the promises in their hearts and live their lives dependent on God's grace.

Mary's actions are more in line with the way of the Spirit.

I am reminded of Lucy in the film Prince Caspian. Lucy is the littlest sibling, the least in the pecking order, but she has a delightful love for Aslan (Jesus) with an accompanying sensitivity to when His presence is near.

In a dream, she is in a scene in the woods, something is drawing her onward, she is seeking. The wind gently stirs, picking up the leaves and causing them to swirl into angelic forms amidst heavenly whisperings and echoes of divine language. Lucy understands this heavenly communication, and she can feel it in her Spirit – Aslan is near. The realms begin to open. She forgets all else to turn her face toward Him, and follow the wind into an encounter of mutual delight – the little girl and the huge lion revelling in each other's company in a gorgeous forest glade.

A little like Mary's love of Jesus.

Lucy's older siblings, however, often condescendingly roll their eyes at what they perceive to be Lucy's little imaginings and childish ways, and struggle to believe her encounters.

A little like the disciples.

Lucy, like Mary, reminds us that it is often the least, the littlest, the marginalised who have eyes to 'see' Christ long before others.[64]

The things of the Spirit are foolishness to the mind of the flesh and cannot be understood by it, thus, as Paul says years later, the message of the cross is foolishness and an offence to the flesh.[65]

The good news, however, is that God's foolishness is wiser than men, and the weakness of God is stronger than men. He delights in taking the foolish things, the weak, the insignificant, the despised things, and displaying His glory through them. And He does it for a reason.

He does it so that no flesh should glory in His presence.[66]

Mary had stepped into this place in the Spirit. She was prepared, as a seemingly quiet and insignificant woman, to make a fool of herself for Jesus. Instead of anointing Him privately, she boldly put her devotion on public display. She gloried in her Lord and in Him alone.

Mary walked through the men in that room with courage, humility, purpose, love, gratitude, boldness and passion. She didn't intentionally make a fool of herself; it just happened as Jesus filled her vision and everything else became dim. She knew who He was, she knew how worthy He was, and she knew she wanted to pour out her devotion on Him.

This type of worship tends to offend, just like the cross.

The cross and this anointing insult the logical mind. They are both an affront; a man who wastes his life on a cross and a woman who wastes a year's wages on him. What a waste of time and money. And wasting time and money are two activities the Western culture finds particularly offensive because time and money are two of our gods. Mary's life confronts these gods head-on.

No wonder Jesus set Mary's anointing as a memorial; we *need* to be reminded.

## Chapter 8

# Hearts

Not only do we need to be reminded and challenged regarding the gods of our culture, but Mary's anointing also challenges our Christian culture. It challenges how we 'do' church.

In recent decades, much discussion has arisen in Christianity about church structure and five-fold gifts - in particular prophets and apostles. The Holy Spirit has gradually restored our understanding of the five-fold roles and their purpose in the church. Unfortunately, along with restoration, there has often come a mistaken repeat of the disciples' same contest… who is the greatest. Not that we would like to admit that. And attention on the five-fold gifts has its place, a crucial place really, as it is the role of these ministries to steward God's flock into wholeness and maturity.[67]

Our experimentations with church structure also have their place, whether we are advocates of megachurch, home church, parachurch, hierarchical or flat leadership models, or the multiple options in-between. Yet, I think we have to be careful not to miss the point, once again.

Mary and her act of devotion is what Jesus wanted to be remembered. If He had wanted a memorial to the role of apostle, or prophet this side of the grave, He would have made that clear. If He had wanted a prescribed, one-size-for-all rule for leadership or church structure, He would have given us that. But He didn't. He gave us some commandments, and He gave us some guidelines… and then He gave us Mary's memorial.

You might be thinking, "what has that memorial got to do with any of the above?" Once again, I simply believe that Mary's memorial points us back to the foundation of our faith, Jesus Christ, and it provides a litmus test for the state of our hearts towards Him.

Whether we are apostles, prophets, teachers, evangelists or pastors, whatever our gift or call, at the core of it all, He is looking for devotion like Mary's. He is looking for worshippers who will waste themselves on Him. Hearts that worship in spirit and in truth. His eyes range throughout the earth to strengthen these ones.[68] Worship is no waste. When you pour out your life in worship to Him, you will be sought, and you will be found.[69] By the One you adore.

Regardless of our gifts and whether we fellowship in a megachurch or a home church, or believe in hierarchical or flat leadership, Mary's memorial brings us back to what the body of Christ is about… and *it is about the heart.*

If there is not the rhythmic beat of a radiant heart of worship at the centre, then it does not matter what external form the church body upholds, it will be spiritually withered. It will be all form and no fire.

Both corporately and individually, the heart of worship is our greatest guard against the pitfalls of our own flesh. A worshipping heart like Mary's is focused on the Saviour, surrendered to His Spirit and obedient to His commands. The ways of the flesh don't get a chance. Instead, gifts are used as sweet offerings back to Christ to bring glory to Him. The externals of form and format are held as secondary things, knowing that these things are not the lifeblood of the church body.

Connection with Jesus is the lifeblood.

Unfortunately, it is uncommon to find believers in the Western church wanting to be like Mary. If we're honest, many of us would rather avoid it because of the reproach and misunderstanding it attracts. Yet, if we only recognised how much this type of devotion means to Jesus, then much of the positioning and striving after recognition would fall away.

A lot of things would then fall into place.

## Love

They would fall into place because Mary embodies the crucial Kingdom principle of love. Jesus himself, told us that the first and greatest commandment was to love Him above all else, with everything we had; all our heart, soul, mind and strength.[70] No wonder He wanted us to remember Mary and her act of devotion because the Greatest Commandment is exactly what she demonstrated. Love of the highest order.

It reminds us to remain devoted to the source of love, Jesus himself. The more we pour out our love upon Him, the more we become like Him because we become like what we worship.[71] As the disciples gradually came to see, we can compare importance or we can go deeper and learn that underneath it all, the greatest thing is love. Jesus did not make a memorial to any of the impressive gifts, talents or calls of his followers; He made a memorial to her outpouring of love upon Him. Mary's devotion is a living example of Paul's 'more excellent way.'[72]

Metaphorically speaking, our Christian lives are a little like a book. If we are living the 'excellent way,' then the greatest commandment, to love God, makes up the front cover of our book, and the second commandment, to love others, makes up the back cover. The front cover and the back cover are each unique, yet they are intrinsically linked and complement each other. These two commandments sum up the Christian walk and hold it all together. What it pays to be aware of, however, is that if one cover is missing, our pages will fall out. Equally, if the covers are on back-to-front, the book will be confusing.

When the covers are in place correctly, the two commandments set a Divine order in our lives and in the church. We ignore this Divine order to our peril. If we let the back cover take the place of the front, then we will love from our own humanistic ways of love, and it will go awry. This will happen subtly at first – without being aware of it, we may love in order get things in return, to feel better about ourselves, to prove ourselves, to feel important, or to be 'good Christians.' In the end, however, this type of love becomes noticeably warped and brings no glory to God. Rather, it draws glory to self. Just like the religious system that crucified Jesus.

The majority of those religious leaders, while spouting their love for God, showed without a doubt, by their lifestyles, that they had their covers back to front. They loved in order to be noticed, and they loved in order to climb the ranks. They loved in order to notch up points with God, and yet they refused to come to God personally. They couldn't recognise Jesus through all the fog of their religious ambitions because their back-to-front covers had them blinded. On top of that, the content of their books didn't match what was touted on the covers. A grand Hollywood façade. The result was that Jesus was a very real threat to their self-loving glory, and they knew it. In the end, their envy of Jesus became so demonically fuelled that they orchestrated his crucifixion.[73] They ushered in death.

In contrast, when there is Divine order, the outcome is life. Kingdom life. Prioritising love for God and guarding this as the front cover, results in loving others from the overflow of receiving God's love for us. When the source of our love is the intimacy of abiding in the vine, our love will become increasingly like Christ's. We will have tapped into a divine artesian spring, and rivers of living water will flow from our innermost being. Our love will be the overflow of Him. It will offer to others the supernatural grace and truth that our Saviour's love offers us.

The source of love is God. We love God, and we love others because He first loved us.[74]

Love God and let Him love us back. From this, love others.

## Fire

With this type of order, Mary calls us back to what is most important and reminds us that it is counterproductive to save people into anything else, including into Christian busyness. They're to be saved into relationship.

Unfortunately, busyness is often the death of relationship, whether with Jesus, friends, or family. We would be wise to remember that cultivating relationship with God is the highest honour of the church. If we create disciples who have hearts like Mary, they will find rest in Christ, and follow where His Spirit leads. Let everything flow from this. Then God will align us in the body as naturally as water contours a riverbed.

The trouble with this good work of Mary's, is that it doesn't quite fit our penchant for achievement. It is not really measurable. Often, we prefer to achieve good works that illustrate we're good Christians and good churches. It's nice to be able to tick the denominational boxes at the end of the year, as evidence that we have been effective: how many outreaches we've had, people we've saved, tithes we've taken, courses we've run, poor we've helped, missionaries we've supported. These are all important, and some of these activities are in direct response to the commands of Jesus.

But Jesus is looking for something more than that.

He's looking for burning hearts. Hearts ablaze with first-love fire for *Him.*

It is all too easy to be so busy we don't notice the fire ebbing. We get distracted from Jesus. We turn away from being Spirit-led. We rely on our own strength, talent, charisma, or organisational skills. We don't want interruptions to our systems. We become a lot like the world, and our love grows cold.

We can lose the cry of Moses; "If your Presence does not go with us, do not bring us up from here."[75] In other words, without your Presence, we're sunk. Moses went on to say that God's presence with them was the defining mark of His people. Without God's Presence, they were no different to the rest of the world. And it's the same today. Without His Presence, we are just another club. We are no different. There is nothing more tragic in the modern-day church than to lose the cry of our first love. To just go through the motions. To lose our fire.

Especially to lose our fire *and not notice.*

Jesus wants followers like Mary. And how do we measure her type of 'following' as an achievement; her sitting at the feet of Jesus, her wasting her wealth on Him in a foolish act? What did that really achieve? What would these things look like on our end-of-year scoreboard? Not so appealing. In fact, there probably wouldn't be a tick box on our end-of-year scoreboard for this type of behaviour. But the thing is, that whatever it achieved, it was right on target in Jesus' viewpoint.

It ticked the box as far as He was concerned, and it received his absolute approval.

It was the *only* work done by any of His followers in the gospels that He described as 'good.'

Perhaps it is time to lay all of our works on the altar and ask for the fire of the Holy Spirit to fall. How much of our Christian activity would be burned up as wood, hay and straw?[76] How much of it is Spirit-led, birthed through intimacy in the secret place, and purely for His glory?

Hidden beneath the complexity of modern Western church life, there remains a simple, radical, passionate, fiery, sold-out, seed of devotion like Mary's.

Perhaps it is time to return to that place.

## Encounter

Perhaps, part of the challenge is that if we have never experienced God's Presence, then we will not know when it is missing. All I know, is that from my own experience of God's manifest presence upon my body, soul, and spirit on the day I was saved, I was left with an indelible imprint of God and of Kingdom realms beyond the physical. It left me with a divine hunger and thirst for more of His exquisite presence. There is *nothing* on this planet like it, and we are designed to hunger and thirst after this. Ultimately nothing else will satisfy.

Nothing.

My senses have experienced Him, and it has forever ruined me for anything less. I have tasted and seen. I am undone by God, and because I have experienced the reality of His presence, anything less remains unappealing.

Perhaps, this could be illustrated as being like the difference between seeing a photo in a recipe book of a scrumptious meal on a beautifully set table, in an exquisite setting, and comparing this to actually *being there* and actually *partaking*... physically sitting at the table, smelling the wafting aromas, savouring the flavours, absorbing the atmosphere of the setting, touching the serving bowls, drinking in the visual beauty. Tasting, touching, smelling, seeing, and hearing. Being there is totally experiential.

In comparison, a photo in a recipe book can only communicate in part. There is more. So much more. The photo points us towards the reality, but it is only a flat two-dimensional image, whereas experiencing the reality is another thing altogether. It is multi-dimensional. You're in amongst it.

It can be like this in our Christian life sometimes. Gatherings that offer the recipe book instead of 'taste and see' experience. Why on earth would we settle for a cold hard recipe book, when God Himself has invited us to "taste and see" that He is good?

A feast awaits!

With reference to God, the Apostle John talked about what the disciples had *heard*, what they had *seen* with their eyes, and what their hands had *handled*.[77] God has not designed this type of experience to be past tense. It did not die out with the disciples. The fact that Jesus memorialised Mary's act, *forever,* is to remind us that this is what He wants *even now.*

He wants encounter. He offers open realms and Kingdom experiences. He wants followers who will push through the crowds to be with Him. And not just once. The encounter I had with Him at salvation was just the beginning, and it has been followed by many others, ranging from times of being totally overshadowed and undone by His Presence, to the more simple daily moments of knowing His presence in my home, workplace and everyday life.

He is just as present with us right now, through His Spirit, as He was to Mary and the disciples when He was in a physical human body. Indeed, He said it would be to our advantage that He go away and come back to us through His Spirit.[78]

He is even more accessible now. To all of us. Worldwide. At all times.

Chapter 9

# Jailbreak

The more we ponder Mary's anointing, the more we discover, and it becomes increasingly clear why Jesus wanted to memorialise this. Mary's one prophetic act, in its timing and actions, resounds with clarity through the ages. It stands as a prophetic signpost, and marks the convergence of ancient paths and new. It picks up on Old Testament symbolism, provides a pivot point just before the crucifixion, and then launches us prophetically into what Jesus died for.

As we saw earlier, Mary's anointing of His body spoke prophetically of His body being given for us and His blood. A deeper layer to this, is that Mary's prophetic act pointed to the fulfilment of the Passover events of approximately 1500 years earlier, which were a prophetic promise of Christ Himself.

Christ the Passover lamb.

Mary's anointing and the Passover are two inextricably linked memorials.

## Escape

Way back in the book of Exodus, the Passover became a memorial feast set by God Himself, to celebrate Israel's supernatural escape from slavery in Egypt.[79] God's people, who had been in slavery for 430 drudging years, escaped amidst spectacular judgements upon Egypt by the hand of God. It was the final judgement upon Egypt which introduced the Passover lamb. This was a sacrificial lamb, whose body and blood for each household protected them from the death of their firstborn. Not so the Egyptians. It was the tipping point for their leader, Pharaoh, and the thrusting out of the Israelites into their exodus. Thus began their journey out of slavery and into freedom.

Now, Mary, with profound timing, in fact about *fifteen centuries to the day* after the original Passover meal, anoints Jesus…on the very cusp of the Passover meal memorial, which was the annual celebration of the Passover.

As John the Baptist had prophetically declared just a few years earlier, "Behold! The lamb of God who takes away the sin of the world!"[80]

The Lamb of God. His body, so beautifully anointed by Mary, was to be the sacrifice for our sin in a whole new journey for God's people, which is often referred to as the New Exodus.

The prophetic timing of her act and of His death is astonishing.

Only God could orchestrate such precision.

In Egypt, around fifteen centuries earlier, the Israelites had become more and more enslaved and shut down. They lost their freedom to worship and were being driven so hard it threatened to destroy them. The ensuing battle between God and Pharaoh was all about worship and it resulted in all the gods of Egypt being trounced and the nation almost destroyed.[81] The One True God was revealed, and God's people were liberated into freedom to worship Him. He carried them out of Egypt and brought them to…*Himself.* [82]

*He* was the goal of the exodus.

In a parallel story, the New Exodus through Jesus' life, death, and resurrection meant liberation for God's followers from the temple system of Israel. It had become a hard and often cruel taskmaster. Jesus changed that. He fulfilled the Law and ushered in the Kingdom of God. The new covenant meant the end of the temple system as the way to worship God.

What had become an empire of mans' rules and regulations, suddenly became obsolete when Jesus died and rose again, the Passover lamb sacrificed once and for all to atone for our sin. No more animal sacrifice. He had provided His own blood for our forgiveness. Done.

He was now the Way, the only Way, into the presence of the Father No more barriers to worship. Immediate access to God. Welcome home.

Only God could orchestrate such parallels:

The exodus out of Egypt was all about worship.

The New Exodus is all about worship.

## Access

Mary, in an extravagant act of worship, provides a practical demonstration of what it's all about, prophetically, before the Lamb is even slain.

When it comes to the crunch, this thing called Christianity might be all about worship.

Our freedom to worship has been won in a spectacular way. Like the supernatural events surrounding the exodus out of Egypt, such as the plagues, the parting of the Red Sea, and the pillars of cloud and fire,[83] the New Exodus was also profoundly supernatural.

Christ's Spirit caused Holy chaos. His victory over death burst out from unseen dimensions and onto public display. The realms were rent asunder by His death and resurrection – the sun vanished for hours, the earth quaked, the rocks split, graves were opened, and the bodies of dead saints rose and walked among the living.[84] And perhaps the most profound thing rent asunder… was the temple curtain. The curtain separating everyone except the High Priest from access into the Holy of Holies. It was now torn in two. From top to bottom. An impossibility, humanly speaking.

But it happened. Now there was no more separating curtain.

Welcome into the Father's house.

Free access to the throne of grace for anybody through faith in the blood of Christ. The Father's door wide open. An open invitation to all. No need for a priest or Pharisee to mediate between God and us.

Jesus had demonstrated this everywhere He walked on planet earth. He loved the least, and He welcomed them to get up close and personal. He delighted in lifting up the down-trodden, binding up the broken-hearted, and befriending the unclean.

Jesus shows us that this was always God's heart, whether in the Old Testament or the new. He always loved us and wanted us to come close. Between the Old Testament and the New, God did not change.

*It is the way we approach Him that changed.*

No more straitjacket of religious oppression full of cunning man-made rules designed to keep the poor and oppressed just that - poor and oppressed. Barricaded from God and enslaved in a parasitic system that kept the religious leaders firmly at the top and feeding off everyone underneath. A system that meant those below were burdened by heavy loads continually made heavier, and then overloaded by the judgement, shame, rejection, and contempt of those same leaders.

In this New Exodus, Jesus orchestrates the most radical jail-break ever. He tips things upside-down – which is why He was, and often still is, so hated. The religious leaders sensed all along that He threatened the security of their religious empire. All they held dear; the well-oiled machinery of the religious system which profited them so pleasingly, did not need Jesus poking a stick in the wheel. Everything ran smoothly and efficiently without

Him. Unfortunately, they just did not comprehend. Jesus was God, and had come to inaugurate His new covenant.

And He loves freedom.

## Freedom

The New Covenant means *free access* to the Father's presence for any who will believe, bow the knee, and follow Jesus. And this is what the Pharisees would never do. They had rejected the baptism of John, and thus had rejected the will of God for themselves.[85] They didn't believe Jesus. They didn't believe His prophet. They didn't want to bow the knee in repentance. And they didn't want any of their followers to, either.

Instead, they chose to remain on their religious pedestals with stiff necks and uncircumcised hearts and ears. They had every physical ritual of circumcision, but hearts of stone, ears that were blocked, and eyes that could not see the things of the Spirit. With relatively few exceptions, they continued as their fathers, always resisting the Holy Spirit and persecuting and killing the prophets.[86] The Spirit offered freedom. They chose control.

In this jail-break, Christ died for us so that we could come with absolute childlike freedom and joy into His presence. Like Mary. So that we could be as one with Him, both on earth and for eternity.

He totally loves our company and delights in relationship with us. He loves to help us. Loves to see us thrive. Loves us to have fun. Loves us to advance the Kingdom. Loves us to love others. Jesus is the way to our Father in heaven who is madly in love with us, interested in every detail of our lives, and *for us.* Jesus is the perfect representation of the Father. They are one. So, we can know that the Father will respond to people in the same way Jesus did during His life on planet earth. Jesus died so we could come home to the Father's house and know the Father as He did. Be His brothers and sisters.

This jail-break out of slavery and into the freedom of worship is gobsmacking good news for 'outsiders.' This whole story is typical of the way

Jesus operated, typical of the heart of God. Jesus constantly seemed to delight in mixing with the 'wrong people' and elevating the humble. He usually tipped the social order on its head; speaking to women, giving time and blessing to children, touching lepers, turning aside for cripples, eating with tax collectors and sinners, inviting criminals into paradise.

The Kingdom of God is often in complete contradiction to the social orders man creates. What society holds up as 'the thing' to pursue, is often at the bottom of the pile in God's Kingdom, and often those people and those acts scorned and rejected by society (and sometimes even the church), are of highest value.

## Contested

The rending of the curtain was not seen as good news to the religious leaders of the day. From that point, began a new onslaught of the flesh against the things of the Spirit. Immediately, the leaders tried to silence the good news and bribed soldiers to lie about Jesus' resurrection.[87]

They attempted to blockade the new free access closed before anyone could get through.

Today the battle still rages; it just looks a little different. Man-made traditions and the flesh still resist freedom in worship. They smother, cover, and control access into the presence of God. Often unintentionally.

Think of the modern Western church. Did we really mean to get so caught up in all the… stuff? Our free access to Jesus slowly buried beneath the responsibilities and busyness of church buildings, working bees, potlucks, fund-raisers, and on and on and on. The more we have, the more it takes to maintain it all. Sometimes, all the bells and whistles become our focus and, in the end, enslave us.

The machinery can become our Lord and Master. Like Pharaoh, it demands more and more, and we bow to its demands of time, money, and in the end, worship. Yes. Worship. Do we really need flash church buildings, even flasher sound desks, polished music teams, plush upholstery, nice carpet, big car parks, more courses and manuals, and coffee machines?

Or do we need a fresh dose of Mary's perspective?

Mary, who cut across all the lesser things and connected with the heart of Jesus. Whose year's worth of wages got lavished on Him. Who refused to let the busyness, and doing, and people, and places, distract her from the one thing of connecting with His heart and ministering to Him.

She just had this knack of cutting right across the grain of things, and hitting the mark. Fiery devotion. Passionate worship. Humble. Listening and following. Perhaps, if we had less stuff and got our focus off all our stuff, we would find the presence of God that many hunger for.

All the time and money spent on the externals of 'worship' and getting it just right…what if Jesus was more blessed by simple hearts in an out-of-tune singalong? I heard a prophetic word at church years ago, which has never left me. It was about corporate worship. The prophetess said she saw a vision of a big spiritual sound desk in the heavens above the church and it was being run by the angelic host. Through this sound desk, all of our worship was filtered. Here it was mixed in a whole different way, and instead of hearing music, *they heard our hearts.*

There can be a major difference between the sounds coming from our mouths and instruments, and what is going on in our hearts.

Don't get me wrong, I love 'in tune' and have been thoroughly blessed by professional Christian music over the years. I still am. It is not right or wrong in and of itself. It is merely another area in which we can get bogged down and distracted by externals - building the machine at the expense of ministering to Jesus in simplicity.

How much of it is actually necessary? What if we just stopped regularly and pondered Mary? What if we did what Jesus said and remembered her - who she was and what she did? Because to Jesus, this is what He wanted; this is what He elevated, held up, honoured as an example of devotion for all time.

~

## Beyond Words

And Mary didn't sing a word.

I am reminded of Hannah's prayer in the book of Samuel. Hannah's lips moved, but her voice was not heard. She didn't say a word. She spoke in her heart, and Eli, the priest, thought she was drunk.[88] But Hannah's soundless prayer is one of the most potent examples of prayer in the Bible. Hers was a total outpouring of the heart and resulted in the birth of Samuel, an incredible prophet who brought the nation back to God.

Likewise, the worship Mary brought was an act beyond words. An overflow of Spirit-fuelled passion straight from the heart. Mary was a living demonstration of the new wine of the New Covenant. And "New wine *must* be put in new wineskins" (Mark 2:22, words of Jesus, italics mine). As Mary's anointing confirms, new wine cannot be contained in old forms. She was totally outside the box of her time.

The old wineskin could not contain her act of worship…so she broke it. The power and extravagance of the worship bursting from her heart was Spirit-fuelled, and she chose to go with it.

She broke the box.

## Chapter 10

# Shame

When a Spirit-fuelled act of new-wine-worship breaks out, it is inevitably costly. Reactions abound. Offence is common and can lead to some pretty intimidating behaviour as we have seen. Behaviour like the murderous hatred of the religious leaders towards Jesus. There is Judas' bitter betrayal of Jesus fuelled by Mary's act. Then there is the harsh criticism, misunderstanding, and shut-down attempts from the disciples towards Mary. These types of reactions can cripple the people they are aimed at.

While that may not be the intention, it is often the result.

When we are on the receiving end of hatred, criticism, betrayal, misunderstanding, shut-downs and put-downs as a result of extravagant devotion, it can easily result in shame. Shame often follows judgement. And judgement is no stranger to religious settings.

Whether intentional or not, judgement can control people's expressions of faith, as shame causes us to want to hide. It can kill freedom, as the fear of man dominates in places where judgement and shame hang out.

Perhaps we have been a Mary in the past. Perhaps we have dared to be vulnerable and express our love for Him freely, but the reactions of others have caused us to shrink back and play it safe. Now we offer worship that fits the box designed by what the majority deems acceptable and hide our true hearts away.

Perhaps we have been like the disciples. Misunderstanding the mess and extravagance of the spontaneous devotion of others, and sharing our offence and criticism vocally and publicly.

Perhaps we have even been like Judas. So absolutely peeved at others' extravagance, that we have set our face against God and His people.

Perhaps we can see parts of ourselves in each response. And perhaps, even now, shame is knocking at our door.

As followers of Christ, no matter how much we have blown it, no matter our weaknesses or failures, shame is not to be our portion. Christ ensures that.

## Trounced

Jesus has dealt with shame. Not because He lived an easy life. Not at all. In fact, completely the opposite. During His sojourn on planet earth, He was called everything from demon-possessed to insane, and He copped more than His fair share of complaints and criticism.[89] He was hated without cause and constantly misunderstood.

His death on the cross had enough shame attached to bury most people. Put yourself in His place: publicly stripped naked, abused, beaten, tortured, condemned, humiliated, mocked, spat upon in the face, dressed up and taunted, bearing the stigma of a criminals death, betrayed and deserted by

His followers, rejected, hated, misunderstood, physically marred beyond recognition, bodily weak, and scorned by the religious leaders, as his life ebbed from Him.[90] The life and death of Jesus were crammed full of opportunities for shame to lord it over Him. But despite all this, in typical Jesus-style - shame got trounced.

Instead of coming under shame from this onslaught and from the scorn of the 'important people,' Jesus once again turned the tables…

*Jesus scorned the shame.*

The book of Hebrews says, He "endured the cross, scorning the shame." (Heb 12:2, NIV) He scorned it. Despised it. Shame had nothing on Jesus. He was not coming under any attempt of man or the devil to shrink Him. He was a servant King, yes, but He bowed the knee to the Father's agenda alone.

He turned shame's agenda back on itself.

## Spirit of Christ

We get an amazing insight into this from Isaiah 50:6, "I did not hide My face from shame and spitting." These words are astounding. Though they are written in the first person by Isaiah, it is not Isaiah they are referring to, but Jesus. The Spirit of Christ is fore-telling His story through the prophet over 600 years beforehand in this portion of scripture, sometimes referred to as the third "Servant Song." It is about Jesus. And here the Spirit of Christ tells us of the sufferings He would experience in His death. The Spirit of Christ was in the Old Testament prophets centuries before Christ's appearing. He told his story to them beforehand, and this is what we see here.[91]

Another example of the Spirit of Christ at work is how Moses, the prophet whom the Lord knew face to face,[92] could consider the reproach of Christ as greater riches than the treasures of Egypt.[93] Yet Moses lived approximately 1500 years *before Christ!* How could he value the reproach of Christ before it had even happened? The Spirit of Christ revealed to him the sufferings and the glories that Christ would experience. So, by faith, Moses chose to look ahead to the reward, to the glories of Christ, and made life choices accordingly – He chose to suffer with God's people, slaves at the time, rather than pursue the treasures of Egypt which were at his fingertips. By this faith, the prophet led the exodus out of Egypt.

The story of Christ is woven into the Old Testament in the voices of the prophets. Their witness of Jesus, centuries and even millennia before Christ became man, is perfectly normal when we know that the testimony of Jesus is the spirit of prophecy.[94] Jesus is the heart of prophecy.

The profoundly accurate prophecies of Christ by these Old Testament prophets were consistently picked up by New Testament authors and woven afresh into their messages. For example, the Isaiah 50:6 scripture mentioned above in the third "Servant Song," is alluded to three times in Matthew's gospel alone, in his telling of Christ's death. In this way, the Old Testament provides the foundation for the New and brings ancient meaning to the surface, which would otherwise remain hidden.

In this case, the assault of shame.

Isaiah's prophecy, in Isaiah 50:6, says Jesus did not hide His face from shame. He looked shame in the face, eyeball to eyeball, and scorned it and in so doing, He turned the tables on the devil's agenda to ruin humanity. In the Garden of Eden, Adam and Eve, after they'd blown it, realised they were naked, then gave in to shame and hid from God. This is what shame does. It drives us to hide. It mars relational intimacy. It shrinks us. But as Isaiah reveals, Christ, the second Adam, overthrew shame at the cross. He refused to hide. Not from man, nor from God.

Shame had nothing on Jesus, and because of that, it need not have anything on us.

He scorned shame because His identity was totally secure in His Father's love, and His Father's opinion was the only one that defined Him. When we put our trust in Him and find our identity in Him, He graces us to scorn shame just as He did. To put it under our feet and hold our head high. It does not belong to us. No matter what we have done or what has happened to us in the past. Through Jesus, we can scorn shame too.

In some cases, such as in the reactions of the disciples and Judas to Mary, our shame may have been let in through the doorway of pride. Prideful thoughts. Prideful actions. "When pride comes, then comes shame; but with the humble is wisdom."[95] So in this case, before we can scorn shame, we may need to humble ourselves before our Servant King. When we do, we can know He will lovingly receive our humbling with a smile, lavish forgiveness, and warm embrace. Our new-found humility will shut the door that pride had opened, and free us to scorn shame.

So, whether we are a worshipper who has hidden our face due to shame, or a disciple or religious leader now ashamed of our actions and tempted to hide our face, Jesus does not shame us. He will take our failures and weaknesses and in exchange grace us with fresh revelation of who we are in Him, so that we may scorn the shame and become an unfettered, unashamed, uncontainable worshipper.

# Spirit of Grace

The Spirit of grace is the remedy for the judgement of men and shame. Grace flows naturally to the humble, and grace fuels freedom. Worshippers like Mary flourish in an atmosphere of grace. Fortunately for Mary, she was in the presence of Jesus, who is Grace Himself, and He decisively shut down shame's attempts at her. All the judgements in the room were silenced with His authoritative command:

*"Let her alone." (Mark 14:6; John 12:7)*

Oh, how we need His voice in the church today. Leave her alone. All the voices that condemn the extravagant devotion of the Marys. All the voices that complain. Oh, how we need those who are in step with the Spirit of grace and who understand the joy and honour these devoted ones bring to Jesus himself.

We need those who recognise genuine Mary acts of devotion and aren't threatened by spontaneity, mess, and lavish acts of worship, which don't fit the box. Who are willing to suspend judgement long enough to pursue God's opinion on what is happening, and seek to be so in tune with the Spirit, that they know when He is moving on and through someone; when they are able to discern between fleshly attention-seeking acts as compared to God-honouring but never-seen-before outpourings of love. Those who understand that worship is actually about ministering *to Jesus*. It is not really about us and our comfort zones.

I am not advocating for deliberate, gaudy, attention-seeking displays of the flesh in worship. I know they happen, and I am not promoting this type of 'freedom' in worship.

I also know that 'flesh stuff' may happen unwittingly along the way, as we learn to hear His voice and walk in step with the Spirit. The journey of worship is not perfect, and we often learn most through our mistakes. We need to offer one another grace in these cases, and seek to know each other's heart. Is the heart seeking to glorify God? Or to glorify self?

I also know that church leadership can be incredibly challenging as we balance the desire to allow the freedom of the Spirit while still maintaining some form of order, often motivated by the desire that none of the congregation gets hurt. Often, we have the best intentions, but we end up repeating the same responses demonstrated in this memorial.

*We shut down that which we do not understand.*

## Let go

It usually comes back to trust. Do we trust the Holy Spirit? He is, after all, Jesus in our midst.[96] Do we trust Him enough to walk by faith and let go of our temptation to control? Let go of the reins?

- To let go and worship like Mary? Trusting Him regarding the fallout.
- To let go and let others worship like Mary? Trusting Him to give us discernment when needed.
- To let go and let the Holy Spirit hold the reins of our churches and gatherings and

follow where He leads? Trusting that He will lead us into truth not error.

- To let go and trust the ultimate Shepherd who protects the flock and is the ultimate Head of His church? Trusting that He is who He says He is.

These may be hard questions, but they're worth asking.

Yes, Mary was fortunate that Jesus was there. And we are fortunate that He gave us this memorial because we can know for all time His response to this outpouring of extravagant love. His approval is what matters, and if He loves this type of devotion who are we to stop it?

Chapter 11

# Onward

As we read onward from Mary's anointing, we see glimpses of the impact it had on the lives of some of those who were in the room that day.

Judas for a start. The name of Judas will be forever associated with betrayal. His gods destroyed him. Even though he was overcome with remorse after betraying Jesus, it was too late. What he had done he had done, and it would never be erased. He had betrayed the Christ. He had betrayed the one who loved him and who still called him friend, even in the midst of the betrayal.

The words of Jesus which describe the eternal destiny of Judas are sobering: "…woe to that man by whom the Son of Man is betrayed! *It would have been good for that man if he had not been born*"[97] (italics mine). What a chilling verdict from the One who came to give us abundant life. Not only had Judas refused that Life, he had betrayed it.

The heart and actions of Judas are the antithesis of Mary and her actions, and illustrate that sooner or later, one way or another, for good or for evil, we give ourselves over to what we worship. Our deeds reveal our true doctrine and determine our destiny. We reap what we sow. The gods of Judas became his destruction. He lost his money, his reputation, his life, and who can speak of his eternal destiny?

The religious leaders were also destroyed by their gods but in a different way. Even Judas' return to them in remorse for betraying an innocent man meant nothing to them. They were totally unconcerned at the prospect that they might be taking an innocent life, but instead were concerned only about their version of the law and about the money.[98] Their battle to keep control of their religious empire backfired. They were left with an empty system devoid of God's Spirit, who was now to be found inside the bodily temple of each believer and each gathering of such believers, but not in their man-made temple of stone and timber. And what is even more telling, is that they never even seemed to notice. They preferred a dead system to the Spirit of God who went on to sweep multitudes of new believers into the Kingdom and turn the empire upside down.

The disciples missed it at the time, too. The Bible is open about their weaknesses and failings. But the stories of these ones that missed it bring us hope. All of us have missed it at some time. It is the common story of our humanity, and the joy of the gospel is that our 'missing it' does not disqualify us.

The disciples, all of them, went on after Pentecost to become fiery carriers of the Spirit of God until their deaths. And their deaths illustrated that they had listened to Jesus and had taken on board the lesson of Mary's anointing. They had remembered it.

## Eyes Fixed on Jesus

Each one, not only in life but also in their death, became an incredible illustration of Mary's devotion. Each one gave up their life for Jesus in martyrdom, surely the most profound declaration that a Christ-follower can make; that Jesus is worthy of their life being broken and poured out for Him. In the same way as Mary's alabaster jar but at an immeasurably more extravagant cost. Far more than a year's wages, the disciple's very lives were poured out upon Jesus as the most precious fragrance. They all became heroes of the cross in unique ways.

In recent years, there have been more of these heroes and heroines than ever before. Many of our Christ-following brothers and sisters around the world have died as martyrs. Their extravagant and unyielding love for Christ so courageously displayed.

I wonder if Mary had any idea of the costs that followers of Christ would pay down through the ages. I believe she did. And I believe that is also why Christ chose her and her devotion as a memorial. To remind us, over and over again, that Christ alone is worthy. No offering to the King of Kings is too much. No life given in martyrdom is 'wasted.' Death does not have the final say. He is the resurrection and the life. He is worthy.

I believe this is the type of devotional focus we need in this season when worldwide epidemics, terror, wars, quakes, tsunamis and an endless range of other fear-inducing events rock our worlds by the day and by the hour.

These events include the deliberate and ruthless persecution of our brothers and sisters of faith worldwide. An NGO Report released at the end of 2017 concluded that "the gravity of the crimes committed against Christians today is worse than at any other time in history," including the genocide of Christians in various nations and "unspeakable atrocities."[99] The earth reels and writhes under the weight of human sin and the blood of innocents.

It is time, now more than ever, that we need to fix our eyes on Jesus.

As we minister to Him, we keep ourselves in the place of trust, the place of perfect peace - or *shalom shalom.*[100] Conversely, when we fix our gaze on the world, we find ourselves labouring, fretting, distracted, competing for who's the greatest, and becoming stumbling blocks to the things of God.

The capacity to focus on Christ as Mary did, this type of worship, must increase to enable us to stay above the worries, fears and turmoil. Mary is a reminder to keep our minds focused on 'Him who is able' because through Him, every promise of the Kingdom is 'yes' and 'amen.' Our provision is in Him.

More than ever, worship is the key to vibrant faith. Worship that lifts its gaze above men's opinions, misunderstandings, religious busyness and control, opposition, and persecution, and focuses on the King of Kings.

This level of devotion, I believe, is the most potent form of spiritual warfare available to us in these days. This type of worship causes laughter to roll from our bellies as the devil does his best to take us out, this type of worship causes us to release extravagance when lack wants to stifle us, this type of worship lifts up our heads and bestows glory on us even amid the attempts of the world and the flesh, and at times, the church, to shame us. This type of worship refuses to be intimidated, silenced, or shut down.

*This type of worship knows that whatever is given or given up for Jesus is not a loss. Never a waste.*

It sets before us again the challenge that always accompanies the gospel; are we prepared to let go of the reins? Mary was prepared to release Him. To let Him die. She was also prepared to let herself die in many ways, and let go of her money, her reputation, and her future. Jesus says in John 11:25, that He is the resurrection and the life. She trusted this. As a result, this memorial was made to her on earth. Who can guess what honours awaited her in heaven?

She gained far more than she ever gave up, and this will always be the way for worshippers like Mary.

## Heart Connection

Mary demonstrated the goal of the gospel. People who will "waste" themselves on Him in reckless and extravagant ministry *to* Him. *Connecting* with Him. *Relating* to Him. This relational heart connection with God, the connection of true worship, is the lynchpin of the Christian life, and facilitates ongoing and deepening friendship with God.

Mary was deliberate and focused, and she came right to where Jesus was. She was totally at home getting in the personal space of Jesus. Think of Lucy's huge cuddles with Aslan.

In contrast, the religious leaders of Jesus' day were happy to search the scriptures to find eternal life, but they were not willing to actually come to Jesus. They kept their distance. They preferred the recipe book. In their ongoing complaints to Jesus about His disregard for their man-made rules regarding healing on the Sabbath and mixing with sinners, they consistently demonstrated that their traditions mattered more to them than relationships whether that relationship was with God or with people.

They illustrated intellectual knowledge about God as opposed to the relational knowing of Mary. Mary and Jesus knew each other. The vast majority of the religious leaders refused to pay the price of that path. They held onto what mattered most to them; the rules and traditions of men, and their status. They refused to let these things die. Mary gave these things up.

Mary's memorial brings us back to the reality of His Presence. In the midst of the multitude of things we could do as Christians and as churches, and most of them good things, this memorial centres us. It provides a spiritual plumb-line of the state of our hearts towards Jesus.

Does His presence mean much to us? Or can our lives and churches run smoothly and efficiently *without* Him, thank-you-very-much? Sometimes we've wandered so far from the main thing that we don't even realise the main thing is missing.

Love for God first. *Everything* flows from this. The lifeblood of our faith lies in relational connection. He is the vine; we are the branches. If we are not connecting, we are not living the life He died to give us.

I love the holy wildness of Mary. Whatever our response to her story, may her memorial be as contagious as Jesus intended it to be, and may we allow His own words to be the greatest authority on the type of devotion He is looking for.

*He is worthy.*

# Endnotes

## Chapter 1

[1] J. Ramsey Michaels, *The Gospel of John* (NICNT; Grand Rapids: Eerdmans, 2010), 666.

[2] Luke 10:38-42.

## Chapter 2

[3] Matthew 20:17-19.
[4] Matthew 2:16; Matthew 4: 1-11; Mark 11:18 and many others.
[5] Matthew 23: 1-39.
[6] Matthew 24:3.
[7] Matthew 26:2.
[8] Matthew 23:1-36.
[9] John 8:44.
[10] T. Omiya, 'Leprosy,' *DJG*, 518.
[11] As told in Luke 10:38-42.

## Chapter 3

[12] Michaels, *The Gospel of John*, 666.
[13] https://www.stats.govt.nz/topics/income (accessed June 2020)

## Chapter 4

[14] Ezekiel 1:28; Daniel 10: 8-15; Isaiah 6:1-5; Revelation 1:17; Ezekiel 3:15; Acts 9:9.
[15] Mark 10:35-45.
[16] Matthew 26:40.
[17] Mark 14:50; Matthew 26:31.
[18] John 18:10; Mark 14:52.
[19] John 12:6.
[20] Matthew 26:15; Exodus 21:32.

## Chapter 5

[21] Genesis 2:9; Exodus 28:2.
[22] John 4:23.
[23] Matthew 23:27.
[24] Matthew 16: 16, 17.
[25] 1 Samuel 16:7.

## Chapter 6

[26] Matthew 17:1, 2; Mark 5:37; Matthew 26:37.
[27] Luke 10:17.
[28] Exodus 12:14; 28:12.
[29] Genesis 35:14; Joshua 4:6, 7.
[30] 2 Timothy 3:16, 17
[31] John 21:25.
[32] D. Carson ed et al, *New Bible Commentary* (4th ed. Downers Grove, IL: IVP, 1994), 939.
[33] Matthew 24:14.
[34] Luke 22:19; 1 Corinthians 11: 24, 25.

## Chapter 7

[35] Matthew 16:23.
[36] Ibid.
[37] Michaels, *The Gospel of John,* 670.
[38] John 11:43,44
[39] 1 Samuel 1:3; Matthew 26:53; Revelation 19:14.
[40] Luke 24:50.
[41] John 11:1.
[42] 2 Chronicles 20: 21, 22.
[43] Matthew: 27:26.
[44] Matthew 27:29; Isaiah 50:6.
[45] Matthew 27:28, 29, 35; & 26:67.
[46] J. Dennis "Death of Jesus,' *DJG* 2013, 173-4.
[47] John 6:51.
[48] Luke 22:19.
[49] I. Marshall, ed et al, *New Bible Dictionary,* (3rd ed. Illinois: IVP, 1996), 49.
[50] Ibid., 961.
[51] Exod 29:7; Ps 133:2
[52] Matthew 2:2
[53] John 1:49
[54] Psalms 24:8-10
[55] Jeremiah 10:10
[56] Mark 1:15
[57] Carson ed et al, *New Bible Commentary, 939.*
[58] Joel B. Green, *The Gospel of Luke. The New International Commentary on the New Testament* (Grand Rapids: Eerdmans, 1997), 352.
[59] John 14:9.
[60] Romans 8:8
[61] Luke 4:42, 43; John 6:15; Luke 23:9; John 8:1; Luke 9:11; 19:5.
[62] John 3:8.
[63] John 7:39.
[64] Green, *Gospel of Luke*, 661-665.
[65] 1 Corinthians 1:18-25.
[66] 1 Corinthians 1:29.

## Chapter 8

[67] Ephesians 4:11-16.
[68] John 4:23; 2 Chronicles 16:9.
[69] Acts 13:22.
[70] Mark 12:30.
[71] 2 Corinthians 3:18.
[72] 1 Corinthians 12:31.
[73] Matthew 27:18
[74] 1 John 4:19; John 13:34b
[75] Exodus 33:15.
[76] 1 Corinthians 3:11-15.
[77] 1 John 1:1-3.
[78] John 16:7.

## Chapter 9

[79] Exodus 12:14.
[80] John 1:29.
[81] Exodus 7:16 (TLB); Exodus 12:12; 18:11
[82] Exodus 19:4.
[83] Exodus chs. 7-14.
[84] Luke 23:44; Matthew 27:51-53.
[85] Luke 7:29-30.
[86] Acts 7:51, 52.
[87] Matthew 28:11-15.
[88] 1 Samuel 1:13.

## Chapter 10

[89] John 7:12; 8:48; 10:20.
[90] Matthew 27:26-44 & 26:67; Mark 14:43-15:32; Isaiah 52:14 (NIV).
[91] 1 Peter 1:10, 11.
[92] Deuteronomy 34:10.

[93] Hebrews 11:25, 26.
[94] Revelation 19:10.
[95] Proverbs 11:2
[96] 2 Corinthians 3:17

# Chapter 11

[97] Matthew 26:24.
[98] Matthew 27:3-10.
[99] S. & G. Gallen, 'Persecuted and forgotten,' *Voice of the Martyrs*, November 2018, 2.
[100] Isaiah 26:3

# About the Author

Gillian has a deep love for God. Her adventure of following Jesus began 30 years ago, and over this time she has enjoyed Christian community ranging from local church to parachurch, and home church. She feels privileged to have shared her faith journey with Rowan, her husband of 37 years. They reside in a small coastal town in the Bay of Plenty, New Zealand, where they raised their three children. Gillian enjoys creation, including getting out in the surf, and walking her local bush tracks.

*A Beautiful Thing* is her first book.

www.ingramcontent.com/pod-product-compliance
Ingram Content Group UK Ltd.
Pitfield, Milton Keynes, MK11 3LW, UK
UKHW020223250726
13967UKWH00001B/158

9 780473 531867